Port Carlisle
– a history built on hope

Harriet Pears

This book is dedicated to the memories of everyone contained within it.

Introduction

There are some excellent books about aspects of life along the Solway coast, from its geology to its place in Roman history, to technical descriptions of sailing vessels, to compilations of old photos and postcards.

This book focuses more on a few of the people who lived, laughed, loved, mourned and died in or near Port Carlisle. Some of them are on my family tree, others just 'caught my eye' during my family history research as having a story worth telling.

It certainly doesn't aim to be a definitive history of the canal or railway – the intricacies of which could each fill a couple of volumes. It aims to give an outline of both: their rise, their fall and the factors that influenced them – and the people who brought it all about.

(There is also plenty of scope for someone else to write a book about fishing and chart ALL the legal cases arising from disputes relating to it. It would be a daunting challenge and I wish anyone who undertakes it the best of luck and a lot of a patience).

It includes stories of adventure, bravery, tragedy, determination – and even a possible connection with Jack the Ripper!

This book, above all a story of hope – dashed repeatedly, in the case of the canal, the baths, the railway, but surviving in the name of the one remaining pub.

Contents

Chapter 1 What's in a name?

Chapter 2 The canal

Chapter 3 The wet dock that never was

Chapter 4 The railway

Chapter 5 Silloth, the new port of Carlisle

Chapter 6 Cut off entirely (the viaduct)

Chapter 7 A few statistics

Chapter 8 Beside the seaside

Chapter 9 Not so fine and Dandy

Chapter 10 Manure

Chapter 11 The salmon saga

Chapter 12 This and that

Chapter 13 Peter Irving

Chapter 14 The Irving ships

Chapter 15 Peter John Irving

Chapter 16 Jeffray Peat senior

Chapter 17 Jeffray Peat junior

Chapter 18 Elizabeth Simpson

Chapter 19 The Peat twins

Chapter 20 Pattinson Lawson

Chapter 21 Westfield House

Chapter 22 And finally...

1

What's in a name?

HOP ON the 93 bus from Carlisle today and you'll likely be joining a mix of residents of a string of villages from there to Anthorn, along with ramblers heading for the start of the Hadrian's Wall Walk, at Bowness-on-Solway.

The walkers who pass through Port Carlisle may find it hard to imagine this little village ever was worthy of the name 'port'.

Yet in its heyday, it was heavily involved in trade with Liverpool, and Belfast, and boasted 'hot and cold baths' to attract holidaymakers and day-trippers.

Its rise and fall as a port is the story of just a few decades.

It's also the story of some of the families who lived there during those 'heady' days.

'Port Cumberland'

It is well-recorded that prior to 1819, there was no 'Port Carlisle' – just a hamlet known as Fisher's Cross (or Fiza's Cross), which comprised Kirkland House farm and The Binnacle inn.

The inn was used by Sir Walter Scott as a meeting place for Redgauntlet in the novel of that name (in the novel, it becomes Joe Crackenthorpe's pub: 'a large scrambling assemblage of cottages attached to a house of two storeys').

In fact, 'the Binnacle' was used as an alternative name for the hamlet, even after it had started to grow.

The idea of changing the name to Port Carlisle was suggested in 1823 (*see the chapter on the canal*).

Other suggestions were 'New Port Carlisle'; 'Port William', and; 'Port Cumberland'.

However, shipping reports in 1830 refer to vessels 'arriving off Binnacle', and death notices and parish records also use 'the Binnacle' in the mid-1830s that I know of.

A report in the *Carlisle Journal* in August 1833, praises the welcome (and unnamed hostess) of an unnamed new inn at Port Carlisle. It also deals with the name, starting by saying 'at a place formerly known by the name of the Binnacle'. It goes on: 'This place has hitherto been indifferently called Bowness, Binnacle, and the Canal Mouth'. It goes on to say that the canal company has resolved to call it Port Carlisle, to end all the confusion. And that with other premises built and more projected, it will soon be a pleasant and handsome village.

Maybe the message didn't get through to everyone. Maybe the 'problem' was that it was the canal company (Carlisle men) who wanted the new name, rather than people actually living along the Solway coast. But while the census enumerator in 1841 used 'Port Carlisle,' there are people in 1845 still giving their address as 'Binnacle' rather than Port Carlisle (they couldn't all be living in the pub!).

Just to confuse things, by the 1851 census, Kirkland House is listed as Drumburgh.

Oh, and prior to the canal being built, there are references to 'the port of Carlisle' – meaning Sandsfield.

As an example

John Peat and Elizabeth (née Simpson) are listed in the St Michael's registers as being 'of Bowness' until 1833.

John is described as:

•   1833. Of Fisher's Cross, carrier, when son Jeffery baptised.

•   1835. Of Fisher's Cross/Binnacle, carrier, when son Thomas baptised.

•   1836. Daughter Rachel II died at The Binnacle.

•   1836. Carrier at baptism of twins, Port Carlisle.

Some puzzles…

I've read that Hesket House (formerly the Steam Packet) was built around 1780. If that is so, why does it not feature with the Binnacle and Kirkland House in descriptions of the original hamlet?

Also, given there was no such thing as a steam packet (ship) until the early 1800s, what was it called before? It only makes sense as a name after the opening of the canal.

It is also said that the Hope and Anchor opened in 1829.

However, a notice in the *Carlisle Patriot* in November that year reads:

To let for a term of years, from Candlemas next. That old established public house known by the sign of the Hope and Anchor, situate at Binnacle, in the parish of Bowness, with any quantity of land from 20-80 acres. now in the occupation of Jeffrey Peat.

If it had only been open a few months, why is it described as being 'old established'?

Fishers' Cross seems simply to have been a place where fishermen crossed the firth, except why was it alternatively Fiza's Cross (circa 1800)?

And what about Knock Cross?

2
The canal

Its story may seem one of failure, but that is only one side of things

WHAT CAUSED Fisher's Cross/Binnacle to grow was the building of the Carlisle Canal, to connect the city by water (via the Solway) to Liverpool.

In 1819, a harbour was built at Port Carlisle, with the canal opening in 1823.

The canal was only to last 30 years, when it was replaced by a barely more successful railway, but by then, Port Carlisle had grown from two dwellings to about 80.

Wordy and worthy

In October 1817, engineer William Chapman (1748-1832) produced 'an actual and accurate survey and plan of the best line for a canal between Carlisle and Knock Cross, or Fisher's Cross, and an estimate of the expense of making and completing such a canal for vessels of not less than 70 tons burthen' (source: *Mr Chapman's Report on the Proposed Canal Navigation between Carlisle and Solway Frith. March 1818*).

He'd drawn up a previous report in 1807, but the idea hadn't been taken up. Chapman's original ambition was for a further canal to extend from Carlisle to Newcastle (however, within a year of the Carlisle canal opening, he'd decided the longer stretch would be better served by a railway).

William initially explained (in the 1817 report) why a canal was needed in the first place.

He pointed out that traders from Liverpool, Whitehaven, Glasgow and elsewhere currently loaded/unloaded their vessels at Glasson Lane Foot, with the rest of the 10.5 mile journey to/from Carlisle being undertaken on land.

'*The expense of the line suggested, with its weirs, locks, excavations, towing paths, purchase of land, etc, I cannot venture to approximate further than to say, that, if the rising commerce and manufactures of Carlisle did not demand the superior advantages of a direct communication to the different ports from which it obtains its supply of West Indian and American produce, and of grain in times of scarcity, and for its general exports, including its agricultural products when redundant; the forming of a navigation from the Solway Frith up the Eden would, notwithstanding its disadvantages, be worthy of attention.*'

One can only hope he didn't have to read that 99-word sentence out loud to the committee!

William went on to say that the Solway 'to a given extent above Bowness' was capable of taking vessels of 400 tons laden, quoting evidence given for his 1807 report by pilots Jonah Ashburner, Joseph Liddle, and Jonathan Sims, backed up in 1817 by William Gaddes, master of a Solway trader (ship).

Jonah Ashburner, was 80 (in 1807) and late owner of the sloop Whale. He'd been navigating the Solway since he was 17 and hadn't known any vessels lost but through mismanagement. Jonathan Sims was a pilot from Allonby. William Gaddes had been navigating to/from the Solway for about 20 years (14 of them as master of a trading vessel).

Joseph Liddle/Liddell was a Bowness pilot, who'd known the firth for 30 years. He told William that while the channel was liable to change, it wasn't a problem for those who navigated it constantly.

Other answers were given, in 1817, by: Andrew Milroy, master of a trading sloop; Henry Askew, a Bowness resident who had commanded a Solway trader; Ralph Pickering, an owner of trading vessels; Edward Rowland, a Carlisle timber merchant; Joseph Askew, of Bowness; and Richard Lawson of Drumburgh, 'tide-surveyor of the Customs'.

The best spot

William said the next consideration was where the canal should join the Solway.

Drumburgh Creek would have made the canal two miles shorter, but was deemed unsuitable – it looks as though sand banks were the reason. Other candidates were Cardurnock, and Skinburness.

There were some advocates for it to extend to Maryport – and even Workington or Whitehaven. But William pointed out the obvious: having a canal running for many miles parallel to the navigable Solway would have been a pointless expense.

He ruled out Cardurnock and Skinburness as not only more expensive due to length, but also because they would require costly structural works at the entrance. Cardurnock was exposed, and less accessible than Fisher's Cross. Skinburness beach was steep and would need much excavation to admit vessels at all tides.

He then outlined the situation at Knock Cross and Fisher's Cross, and proposed the canal entrance should be a few yards east of Binnacle House.

One interesting line is that the inner basin and lowest level of the canal would be 16 feet above the lowest neap tides: "nearly on the level of the memorable tide of January 25, 1796, as shewn to me on the walls of Binnacle House."

This tide, 'propelled by a gale,' had destroyed crops and hedges, but it wasn't the highest to have washed over the area. 'A great tide, about a century ago' was said to have been two feet higher still, and to have 'inundated a vast extent of country'. Glasson had been turned into an island, Drumburgh into a peninsula.

William Chapman estimated the canal, as he proposed it, would cost £71,188 to construct. It took four years to dig, including eight locks, and appears to actually have cost £80,000.

Put the flags out and pass the cake

When the canal opened, in March 1823, William Halton, a leading shareholder, proposed Fisher's Cross be renamed Port Carlisle (as I've said elsewhere, it took a while to catch on, and other suggestions were 'New Port Carlisle'; 'Port William', and; 'Port Cumberland').

More than 20,000 people attended the official opening, with most shops in Carlisle closing so owners and staff could take part in the occasion. In fact, Carlisle was reported to be almost deserted.

There were bands, flags, 'wine and cake, by ticket only,' and 21-gun salute before a small flotilla of ships made the official maiden voyage, with people lining the banks to watch.

There were even souvenirs made. In April 1880, an Industrial, Art and Curiosity Exhibition was held at Longtown. Among the 'curiosities' (one which 'told a tale') was a punch bowl with the words inside: 'Let Port Carlisle flourish'.

A great start

The canal was an instant commercial success, and a few weeks after the opening, an advert in the Carlisle Patriot sought: 'Wanted to purchase, two shares in the Carlisle Canal Navigation, for which £25 per share will be given.'

It was also reported that Mr T Gaddes had made three round trips from Carlisle to Liverpool in the few weeks since the canal opened – when eight to ten such voyages a YEAR had been considered the average before.

However, the annual meeting of the canal company in July 1824 was more downbeat. One problem was that half the capital required to build it had been borrowed, and paying the interest had meant the shareholders weren't able to take any dividends for themselves.

Steam to Liverpool and Belfast

Aboard the Carlisle and Liverpool Steam Navigation Company's large and powerful steamer

The Newcastle

Capt Thos Burton

Sail between Port Carlisle and Liverpool, calling at Annan and off Whitehaven (weather permitting) at the following times: –

FROM LIVERPOOL
September 30, October 7, October 10, October 14, October 21, October 24, October 28.

FROM PORT CARLISLE
September 28, October 5, 9, 12, 19, 23, 26, and November 2.

Fares to Liverpool – Cabin 12s, deck 5s. No steward's fees.

And between PORT CARLISLE and BELFAST at the following times: –   From Port Carlisle October 2, back October 3. Over October 16, back October 17. Over October 30, back October 31.

To Belfast – Cabin 10s, Steward's fees 2s, Deck 3s.

Freights are moderate. All suspicious packages shall be given up to the Excise.

J Carruthers, Steam Packet office, Carlisle

The gross receipts of the canal for the year to June 1825 were £2,015 12s 6d. Some 17,755 tons of shipping had used the canal in the same period. And shareholders were assured the prospect of them receiving dividends in the future was bright.

The assurances were premature. Possibly not helped by the vagaries of the weather: at times, the canal didn't have enough water in it for larger ships, and in January 1826, a 'severe frost' put it out of action for a week: quite simply, it froze. Ships sailing up the Solway could be held up by a lack of wind.

The Canal Company then bought a second-hand passenger boat, for £250, for pleasure trips from Carlisle 'to Fisher's Cross' (the old name stuck), to boost income.

7

'Things will get better'

At 1826's annual meeting, the shareholders were again told 'sorry, no dividend this year'. Not only that, but the committee 'reluctantly' wanted to borrow another £12,000 for repairs and other works. This would take the debt to £33,000.

Asked if the circa £3,000 income was enough even to cover the interest, the committee assured shareholders the past year had been the worst they'd ever see.

1828's annual meeting was 'confident' the canal would soon become profitable for shareholders 'at no distant period'. Meanwhile, it was generally believed that the proposed Newcastle to Carlisle railway would be of great benefit to the canal.

1829's annual meeting 'had no doubt' they'd be able to pay a dividend next year.

Not many people turned up in 1833, which was a pity: it was announced that a dividend of one per cent would be paid in October. 1834 saw a similar dividend – but also a further loan taken out, for improvements such as a new bonding warehouse and new dock at Port Carlisle.

The improvements continued, with plans drawn up in 1835 for a new, floating, wet dock at Port Carlisle (likely cost £26,500) (see separate section). This would have enabled steam ships to dock there even at low tide – but at the same time, there were calls for the railway to be extended from Carlisle to Maryport, with the Kendal Mercury warning that if this should happen "alas for Carlisle Canal!"

A lifelong rivalry

The pro-railway voices were so loud, a special meeting of the canal committee in January 1836 specifically addressed criticisms of the canal, with the (then) pro-canal Carlisle Patriot publishing the proceedings in lengthy detail.

One point of interest is that since the canal's opening, more than 4,000 vessels had arrived (up the Solway) at the port. That's more than one a day (matched, of course, by departures). Not bad for a tiny village.

Meanwhile, John Marshall of Hallsteads had offered to buy out the canal company's debt of £30,000, to be repaid at the (lower than present) rate of four per cent.

The meeting may have convinced some, but west Cumberland wanted a railway – and wanted its own ports to prosper. And those in favour were happy to deride the canal as 'isolated' and of little advantage to anyone. This antagonism was to continue for the lifetime of the canal, and its railway successor.

The Maryport and Carlisle Railway company, in May 1836, had capital of £200,000. The canal company, a month later, was looking to sort out its debt by either creating new shares, or apportioning the debt among existing shareholders. They'd each be saddled with a share of the debt and interest payments, unless they cleared it. But whichever route was taken, the shareholders would get a one per cent dividend in the autumn.

It's hardly surprising that the catchily named Cumberland Pacquet and Ware's Whitehaven Advertiser (one paper!) was in favour of the railway. It opined, in October 1836, that if the canal were to be converted into a fish pond, its shareholders would be better off than if it stayed a canal. However, the writer kindly said there was no need to shut up the canal, or "of demolishing 'Port Carlisle'," as it could still be used for heavy goods. The ' ' marks round

Port Carlisle suggest the Pacquet didn't think much of the new name.

Ever the optimists

Despite the worries, the canal company remained positive, and awarded a one per cent dividend in 1837 – the price of the shares rose by either 10 per cent or 40 per cent (it's not said what from, and accounts vary) in a few days that September. And a year later, the Carlisle Dispensary was confident enough announce it was going to invest £700 it had received in bequests in the canal company.

The faithful Patriot, a year later, believed the canal was rising in importance, having 'so long remained unproductive'. It was hopeful the canal owners might finally be rewarded for their patience and large outlay of capital. 1838 was the year the Carlisle and Newcastle Railroad opened in its entirety – with the day declared a public holiday at both ends. It was anticipated this would bring extra traffic to the canal and indeed, tonnage had risen 33 per cent compared to the previous year. The accounts showed a surplus of £1,911 8s 3d and shareholders were to get a dividend of three per cent – and in 1839, it was four per cent. Shares were then listed as being worth £40 – figures repeated in 1840/41.

Certainly the figures for coal exports show the railway from Newcastle was a blessing for the canal. In 1836, 5,263 tons of coal had been shipped from Carlisle. In 1837, it was 25,975 tons. This was still modest compared to Whitehaven (401,340 tons and 405,593 tons), but for sure was a huge increase.

Meanwhile, in September 1838, no fewer than five American timber vessels discharged their cargoes at Port Carlisle at the same time – thought to be unequalled by any other port in the country. The low-water problem (for steamships) remained: passengers had sometimes to be transferred

onboard from small boats. But the Carlisle Journal thought a small steamship could be used as both a tug and a less-alarming intermediary for passengers.

Burdened by debt

However, in 1837 the committee was also looking to borrow £10,000 for works to be carried out – maintaining/upgrading the canal cost way more than it made in revenue.

And while the Carlisle and Newcastle Railroad had its pluses for the canal, at least initially, there were ominous rumblings of what would eventually happen.

A letter to the Carlisle Journal in 1841 encouraged the directors of the canal to start a new share launch – to build a railway from Carlisle to Port Carlisle, on the canal bank.

The author, 'AML,' thought it would keep Port Carlisle attractive as a destination for passengers and goods who otherwise "will fritter away by the different new modes of transit".

The share price in February 1843 was still £40, but by June, it had dropped to £25, and in August, had fallen to £17, before rallying to £17 10s.

As a comparison, in May 1844, the canal shares were still £17 10s; the Maryport and Carlisle Railway shares were £45, and; the Newcastle and Carlisle Railway shares were £90 each.

The canal company called a special meeting in December 1844, in order to do what it had proposed (or threatened) in the past: to spread the entire debt of the company out across all the shares. A share listing for April 1845 has the canal shares priced at 00 00 0, and the dividend the same. The shares were more of a liability than an asset.

The Maryport and Carlisle Railway opened fully in 1845, in which year it was also proposed to build a railway from Carlisle to Glasgow via Annan – ie to a port on the Solway coast.

The canal company petitioned against it, but didn't do so in time for it to be officially considered. But a Mr Carruthers, manager of the Carlisle and Liverpool Steam Packet Company, did get a say, and suggested the railway supporters believed the Carlisle Canal would be abandoned if the railway was built, and that Port Annan would supplant Port Carlisle.

Someone signing themselves Huna had a bright idea in December 1845, with an open letter to the canal committee starting 'your canal wants improving' (see the section on the wet dock). One can only assume the company directors' unspoken response to this was: "I wish." While the shareholders may have shuddered at the thought of more borrowing to fund such an ambitious project.

Rumours abound

What the company actually did that month was advertise that it would receive tenders of loans to the extent of £3,000 total, to pay off securities falling in January. They were offering interest at four per cent, with the loan to be secured by mortgage.

They were back in August 1846, this time not specifying a total, merely 'a limited amount of sums not less than £300'.

Curiously, while the share price in November 1846 was still zero, there was a dividend of £7 7s.

Despite this, it was rumoured (at least) early the following year that the directors of the canal company were considering proposals to convert the canal into a railway, with plans and estimates supposedly prepared the the belief that the (£50,000) project would be carried out 'at no distant day.'

It was reported in June 1847 that a large party of directors of the Newcastle and Carlisle Railway had examined the canal, to see if it could be converted.

The canal company AGM took place, as usual, early in July. Shareholders were told the year's profit amounted to £6,033 9s 4d. This meant a dividend of £4 per share – subject to the deduction of £2 7s 3d for interest on the debt that had been offloaded on to the shares. The debt amounted to £52 per share.

The key detail from the meeting is that the committee thought the best way to convert the canal would be to enter into agreement with some of the neighbouring railway companies. They'd drawn up a prospectus (effectively) and submitted it to the directors of different railways. And would call a general meeting, should anything come of this.

Perhaps they should have paid attention to the 'dreaded' Maryport and Carlisle Railway – its shareholders that year were grumbling they'd been led to believe they'd get a handsome dividend, when they were getting nothing, and in 1848, that railway was running at a loss.

In October 1847, the canal company was again seeking loans, this time for sums of £100 minimum, at five per cent interest.

An ill-fated venture

By January 1848, the shares had a stated price again – but it wasn't great news. The share price was £10, but each share had originally cost £50. And the debt attached to each was now £52 10s. If a share was sold, that £52 10s had to be paid. So, if you'd bought a share for £50 some 25 years or more earlier, it was now only worth £10. Maybe the dividends over the years had offset that, but you wouldn't have come out much ahead.

And if you bought a share, it would cost you £62 10s for something that was only worth £10.

The executors of Thomas Hudson, of Roe Hill, who advertised for sale four shares in the canal company may not have been inundated with offers.

A letter-writer to the *Carlisle Journal* in May 1848 mentioned the 'ill-fated Carlisle Canal', and those attending the AGM in July can hardly have been cheered by the opening words, 'in a year of great commercial depression.'

The total income for the year had been £7,299 11s 3d. There was a surplus (profit) of £4,137, 2s 3d. The debt was £75,015, and the interest on the debt was £3,655 19s 6d a year.

The short version was that anyone with redeemed shares (ie ones on which the debt had been paid off) would get a dividend of £2 7s 3d per share. No one else would get a penny.

Meanwhile, 'various circumstances' had put paid to the canal being sold or leased, though the committee would 'not fail to embrace the earliest opportunity of promoting such an opportunity.'

Some of those attending were not best pleased, and argued that they should all be paid a dividend, given the canal had made a profit over the year; that not doing so would harm the canal's public image, and; that its future prospects were good.

The response was that 'in the present situation of our finances' the company needed to keep the small surplus as a reserve. The chairman, William Halton, did not wish to go into details, given the presence of the Press, but he tried to drop hints that a dividend would be a really bad idea.

One of those urging a dividend was the treasurer, Peter Dixon, who thought that as the company had cut its freight charges, its affairs would improve and its revenues rise. He believed there was £1,700 that could be used to make a dividend.

It got to the point where Mr Halton decided to relinquish the chair, rather than put the motion that a dividend be paid out to everyone. The meeting then voted 67 to 38 in favour of a dividend.

It was only after this that Mr Halton said what he'd tried to avoid saying from the chair: that it had been agreed they'd pay the bank £1,800 interest that week. They didn't have the funds available at the moment to make that payment and a dividend. And the supporters of a dividend reckoned all would be well based on what the company's revenues MIGHT be next year?

He refused to take the chair again, or to stand again for the committee – but was re-elected anyway (!), in the hope he'd change his mind later (!).

It was finally decided the dividend should be paid in October, 'to allow time for the requisite arrangements.'

The *Cumberland Pacquet* reported that it had been decided to make a dividend, though it appeared from the statements of one gentleman on the committee 'more honest and prudent than his colleagues' that there were no available funds to pay it.

In the slough of despond

Mr Halton indeed seems to have been wiser than the rest. In September 1848, the *Carlisle Journal* reportedly sadly that the canal was 'in the slough of despond'.

The Journal reported that negotiations had been taking place with 'certain gentlemen connected with the trade of Carlisle,' who were looking to lease the canal. These traders believed that if charges for using the canal were reduced, then a lot more people would use it. They even offered to guarantee the interest payments for three years.

But, for whatever reason, the canal company's directors weren't in favour.

An open letter in October from 'a proprietor' makes it clear why. The short version being: if the canal was profitable, why lease it out (for three years) others to profit from? If it wasn't profitable, why would anyone want the lease?

The writer was scathing of Peter Dixon's 'masterly analysis' at the AGM, saying since then, cutting the freight charges had succeeded only in a) meaning there would be no dividend, and b) jeopardising the ability to pay the interest on the loans.

Leasing the canal (say to one of the shipping companies) might result in the interests of some traders being prioritised at the expense of their rivals – which would drive away the latter from using the canal and from Port Carlisle.

This would bring it 'to its death throes,' with birds of prey circling as over a dying camel in the desert.

William Halton had by then made it clear he really wanted out, so a special meeting was held in October 1848 to fill his, and another committee vacancy.

Acting chairman William Marshall MP said in the summer, Peter Dixon had told him a project was afoot to lease the canal to him and certain others (including Mr Carr – presumably of the biscuit firm). He had reluctantly gone along with the idea, but it had come to nothing acceptable for either side.

The chairman warned that the railways were pressing manufacturers to give them their trade, and if the canal proprietors didn't make an effort, they'd lose business.

Committee member John Dixon said the canal was in a critical position because of the railways, but had the advantage of being cheaper. He thought Carlisle could become superior to any port on the west coast.

Dixon said he'd wanted to cut the freight charges, but had been over-ruled.

He feared there would be more committee elections soon, given how divided the committee were over the options – and they needed a plan soon that they could put to shareholders.

Still hoping for better 'next year'

The annual report, in July 1849, said the committee regretted it couldn't report as favourably of the condition and prospects of the canal as in some former years!

In fact, the revenue in the bank amounted to just £258 7s.

No dividend, then, but they hoped things would be better the following year.

The new chairman, William James, said he had no good news for those present, and affairs of the Carlisle Canal Navigation Company weren't as flourishing as desired. The only consolation wasn't it wasn't their fault. All traders had suffered from 18 months of poor trade, due to the unsettled state of other countries. Plus, they now had four railway companies competing with them. AND Port Carlisle harbour was clogging up with sand, preventing larger vessels from entering – this was due to a jetty built five years earlier by (the second) Lord Lonsdale at Raven Bank.

Sabotage or coincidence?

Twelve months later, a frustrated William James said had the jetty been built by a poor man, it would have been pulled down long since. But, unfortunately for the company, neighbourhood, public and traders, it belonged to a rich and powerful man.

He got as close as he dared to suggesting the earl was deliberately being obstructive, in order to benefit his own interests at Whitehaven. After all, 'everyone admitted' the jetty did no earthly good to his lordship, and actually did mischief to his own land.

A Canal Shareholder defended the earl, in a letter to the pro-Lowthers Patriot (veering completely off the point by blaming the canal's problems on the railways taking trade and saying surely *that* wasn't Lord Lonsdale's fault?).

His lordship rejected the complaints. In 1854, he was to openly come out against the interests of the upper Solway harbours, but for now, he kept his pro-west coast ports partisanship unspoken – even if many did suspect he was quite happy for Port Carlisle to sand up.

Any hope that reducing freight charges would save the day was desperation. A year later, William James admitted that due to competition from the railways, they'd had to cut charges further, so as not to lose the trade altogether. This hadn't been offset by an increase in trade.

Meanwhile, Lord Lonsdale was digging his heels in over the jetty, which was so harming Port Carlisle.

However, 'now that the railway bubble is burst,' things might get better.

They didn't.

Remember the Carlisle Dispensary investing in the canal in 1838? In 1851, they reported they had a debenture for £700 and an 1828 promissory note for £100, and all they'd had last year was one payment.

From bad to worse

William James opened the 1851 AGM with a 'painful and unpleasant task'.

The canal was not flourishing, and its days of prosperity seemed numbered. Not only had no dividend been possible since 1847 – they'd now been unable to pay their creditors the agreed four per cent interest, having only managed three.

The bank, in January, had (without telling them) decided not to pay the usual half-yearly interest due on the debentures to the company's creditors. The company had managed to pay half what was due itself.

Cutting freight charges hadn't increased trade, as the railway companies had cut their charges, too.

The company had erected five 'agitators' to try to mitigate the obstruction caused by the jetty.

The annual report, meanwhile, said things had gone from bad to worse. And the committee would welcome suggestions from bondholders on how they could improve things.

Accused of cowardice by a letter-writer to the *Carlisle Journal*, the canal directors decided they would after all take on Lord Lonsdale with a law suit.

Something worked, for Lord Lonsdale finally agreed to remove the Raven Bank Jetty – with amazing results. Already, an 11 feet high sand bank had gone and a five foot bar halved in height. Seven years' build-up of sand gone – and with it, any argument that the jetty was not a problem.

Mind you, removing it cost the canal company £50! And the relief, sandbank-wise, would only prove temporary (*see next chapter*).

A new enthusiasm

Did this help the canal? 'Not enough' is the best answer, for five months later, the canal-loyal *Carlisle Patriot* claimed (based on several sources) the Newcastle and Carlisle Railway Company was about to take it over, and fill it in – as had been mooted six years before. And this time, it was to happen.

The 1852 AGM unanimously resolved that the canal should be converted into a railway with as little delay as possible. And that they should raise £30,000 in stocks to do so.

The committee were now as enthusiastic about a railway as they had been about the canal, pointing

out it took two hours for any passenger vessel to get the 11 miles from Carlisle to Port Carlisle by water. They thought a railway (which would take 20 minutes) would have at least 60,000 passengers a year.

They extolled numerous other benefits, and had 'no reason to doubt' that a railway would be a profitable enterprise.

This would allow them to pay off the canal creditors and pay the shareholders a dividend!

William Marshall promised there and then to invest £5,000 in the stocks, with the Dixon brothers John, Peter and George each saying they'd subscribe £1,000. T Milbourne pledged the same sum. T Nelson and Mr Carr each pledged £300, and G Ferguson £200.

Not everyone was convinced. But that is for another chapter.

The requisite legal notices were lodged by the canal company's solicitors, William and John Nanson, in November 1852.

The Bill to convert the canal went through Parliament in 1853, and the company shareholders approved it in June that year.

No parades at the end

On August 1, 1853, the canal closed, and work started on draining it, for work to start on the railway.

It's tempting to regard the canal as a failure. But perhaps its value lay not in its own financial reports, and more in the service it provided to Carlisle.

For upwards of 30 years, it provided the sole link between Carlisle and the sea, other than roads. And canal boats could carry heavy cargoes in a way horses and carts could not.

It had brought down the cost of coal for the citizens and manufacturers of Carlisle, which had helped the city to grow and prosper. It was said to have saved the city £30,000 in fuel costs in its lifetime.

It had also benefited Carlisle's residents. Before the canal, if you wanted to buy something a shop didn't have in stock, it would take them two or three weeks to get it in for you, by cart.

From the time the canal opened, to such fanfares, to the time it was filled in, trade in Carlisle doubled and the city grew. The population in 1821 was 21,000; in 1851, it was 30,000 – roughly a fifty per cent increase.

There was one final 'dividend' from the canal. When it was drained, in August 1853, there was a big haul of fish and eels, including huge pike estimated to be at least 20 years old.

A few sums

As a footnote, the scheme of spreading the debt across shares, brought in in 1844, was a failure. Only eight shareholders paid the share-attached debt, raising just £1,522 10s for the creditors. No interest was paid on the debt after January 1851. The mortgage debt was about £70,000. In 1852, the company was 'nearly bankrupt' and the railway conversion plan really was the only hope any of the creditors had of one day getting their money back.

The income (not profit) of the canal in its final years was:

(1825	£2,015)
1840	£9,346
1841	£8,287
1842	£7,570
1843	£7,997
1844	£7,837
1845	£9,113

1846	£8,256
1847	£8,761
1848	£7,703
1849	£6,234
1850	£6,053
1851	£4,349
1852	£3,597

As well as the canal and land, the company also owned (at Port Carlisle) a light ship, lighthouse and buoys, th e dock and harbour, a warehouse, a bond vault, and 'various other property', totalling around £13,000 in value. It also owned 18 lock and bridge-keeper's cottages, 48 acres of land used as a reservoir, 20 acres of building ground at Carlisle, and other assets and property totalling more than £58,000 – not counting the 100 acres occupied by the railway.

Carlisle Canal: dramatis personae

William Halton

Born circa 1776. Died 1857

It's down to William that Fisher's Cross was renamed Port Carlisle.

Given that he was involved in the canal from the start, he has to have been born in the 1700s. The only candidate on the 1851 census is master cotton spinner, aged 75, living at 44 English Street with wife Mary (née Dobinson, married 1811). It does look as though William Halton's son Charles became a clerk, in 1843, to solicitor William Nanson. William died aged 81, in 1857. Where he was in 1841 is a puzzle.

I have a copy of an agreement between the canal company and the steam navigation company sent jointly by him (as chairman) and a George Thompson (clerk). However, as the 'signatures' seem to be in the same hand as the rest of the letter, I suspect George signed it off for both of them.

Peter Dixon of Holme Eden
Born 1789. Died 1866

In 1851, at Holme Eden, Warwick Bridge, Peter Dixon is 61 and a cotton manufacturer and magistrate. Born in Whitehaven, the census says he also owned 662 acres of land.

After his wife, Sarah Rebecca (née Clarke, aged 55), five adult children, one daughter-in-law, and a visitor, there are 11 servants.

Today converted into apartments, Holme Eden is a 'calendar house,' with 365 windows, 52 chimneys, 12 corridors and four floors for the four seasons.

The mansion was built in 1833-37 for Dixon, it apparently even had stables in the basement with a tunnel running under the garden to allow carriages access to the central courtyard.

The depression in the cotton trade forced the family to sell it in the mid-1870s and it may be known to many as Holme Eden Abbey, having been a nunnery from 1921 to 1983.

Peter Dixon had the cotton works at Warwick Bridge and in 1836, opened a large factory in Carlisle: Shaddon Mill.

The now Grade II* Listed Dixon's chimney is arguably the most-famous landmark in the city, given that at 270ft high, it can be seen from many miles around.

Peter was mayor of Carlisle in 1837-38.

Peter died in 1866 – one of the executors was John Nanson, the solicitor. His effects were initially recorded as 'under £40,000,' but were revised in 1879 to 'under £7,000' – presumably because his company, Peter Dixon and Sons, had gone bankrupt in 1872.

His widow Sarah died in Ambleside in 1875. She was born in Madras, India, they'd married in 1820 at St Pancras Parish Chapel, Middlesex, and in 1871 was still living at Holme Eden.

John Dixon

Born 1785. died 1857

Peter's brother John also had a mansion built – at Knells (Houghton) in 1824

Much of the Knells was destroyed by fire in March 1853 – the flames were said to have been visible from 30 miles away and the family and servants lucky to escape with their lives.

John was twice mayor of Carlisle (in 1839 and 1840) and was High Sheriff in 1838. In 1847, he was elected as MP for Carlisle (Whig) but was unseated as a government contractor. He cleared himself of his government contracts and again contested the city but was unsuccessful. He was a director of the company set up to build a railway from the Lancaster and Preston junction to Carlisle in 1844. He married Mary Tirzah Sturdy in 1814.

Tributes were paid to John Dixon at the 1857 AGM of the Port Carlisle Dock and Railway Company (the canal company's successor). Knells was sold in 1880.

George Dixon

Born 1793. Died 1860

Brother of Peter and John. The 1851 census for Seagrove, Leicestershire, has George Dixon, 57, retired cotton manufacturer, born Whitehaven. He and his wife Mary (born Epsom, Surrey) are listed as the brother-in-law and sister-in-law of the rector of Seagrove, Robert Gutch. George married Mary Boucher in 1836. Like his brothers, he was mayor of Carlisle: from 1842 to 1843, and 1848 to 1849.

George Dixon lived at Tullie House – now, of course, the museum and art gallery. The Dixons were the last private residents of Tullie House, and you can see a portrait there of him and his wife, painted in 1854.

George died at Blencogo. He was deputy chairman of the Port Carlisle Dock and Railway Company by then, with a short tribute paid at the 1861 AGM.

William Marshall MP

Of Patterdale Hall. Born 1796, died 1872

(And John Marshall of Hallsteads. 1765-1845)

William's father John owned a flax-spinning and linen business in Leeds.

John was variously a Yorkshire MP, and sheriff of Cumberland, and it was he who offered to buy the canal company's debts at a low rate of interest, in 1836.

Hallsteads, near Watermillock, was built for John in 1815. After he died there in 1845, his estate was put at £1.5m-£2.5m.

On William's 28th birthday, in 1824 his father gave him the estate of Patterdale, which was worth £13,000.

According to a historyofparliamentonline.org, at the general election of 1826, his father, having unexpectedly secured the nomination as the second Whig candidate for Yorkshire, gave William the seat for Petersfield, Hampshire, which he held until 1830.

At the 1830 General Election, he was returned for the venal borough (ie voters were open to bribery) of Leominster (Herefordshire) after a token contest. There was a fresh General Election in 1831, and he was returned for another venal borough, Beverley, in Yorkshire. He didn't seek re-election in 1832 and took a few years out, before standing as 'a radical reformer' in Carlisle in 1835. He held his seat there for 12 years, becoming the MP for Cumberland East from 1847 to 1868.

William married 1828 Georgiana Hibbert (1801-1866). They had six children.

In 1851, he was living in Belgravia, London – at 85 Easton Square – with Georgiana, children John (21) and Elizabeth (20), and ten servants. In 1861, they were living at Patterdale Hall, with three other children and again, ten servants.

William James

Born 1791, died 1861

William James, of Barrock Park, Low Hesket, who took over as chairman in 1849, was another politician. Born in Liverpool in 1791, he was an MP (Whig/Liberal) for Carlisle from 1820-1826, and from 1831-1834. And an MP for Cumberland East from 1836-1847. He was also sheriff of Cumberland, from 1827-28.

He died at Barrock Lodge in May 1861, predeceased by his wife and seven of their 13 children. An enthusiastic champion of the Port Carlisle railway, he was the company chairman by then, and his loss was lamented at the 1861 AGM.

William Nanson

Born circa 1791/1796. Died 1868

William Nanson, the original canal committee secretary, was also Carlisle's town clerk until 1846,

and the civic centre has a portrait of him, painted by an unknown artist. A listing for the painting says he became town clerk in 1818, and when he resigned, he said he'd taken the role when he was 22 (ie he was born circa 1796).

William resigned as town clerk in 1846, citing ill heath. His son John had been acting as his deputy for some time, and was duly chosen by the council to take over, on a salary of £80 a year. John was also to take over from his father on the canal committee, but William continued his legal work. In 1852, he and son John were the canal company's solicitors.

The 1841 census shows William Nanson, solicitor, aged 45, (NOT born Cumberland) and living at 10 Fisher Street, Carlisle, with his (second wife??) Frances (50) and three (presumed) children, including John, aged 20, a solicitor. By 1845 for sure, father and son had a law practice at 9 Castle Street. William had bought the property in Fisher Street in 1817 – aged either 21 or 26.

Unless he was only 15 when John was born, the 1796 date looks a bit iffy! The only marriage to a Frances seems to be 1837, so it looks like a second marriage. I suspect his first wife and therefore John's mother was Elizabeth (née Ferguson). (See also chapter 6).

His age at death, in Carlisle in 1868, is given as 76: ie he was born 1791/2. And the 1861 census gives his age as 69. He was then living in Bloomsbury, Middlesex, listed as a 'solicitor, not in practice,' with wife Frances (also 69, born Carlisle) and a domestic servant. Rewind to 1851 and they are in Cranbrook, Kent, both aged 59. The later censuses show him born in St Clement Danes, Westminster, matching a 1791 birth to a John Nanson and Elizabeth.

The 1851 census shows John Nanson, town clerk and attorney at law, aged 30 and living at the same address (10 Fisher Street), with his wife Caroline Fletcher Nanson (née James, aged 25), son William (1), and four domestic servants. John and Caroline had married in Taunton in 1847.

Jonah Ashburner

The veteran Solway navigator died in Allonby, late in 1819, aged 92. A Jonah Ashburn married, in Bromfield in 1750, a Hannah Thornthwaite.

The Askews

Joseph and Henry Askew, of Bowness, show up together on the 1841 census. Henry was then 56, so born about 1785, and Joseph was 20 years older. Henry is listed as a sea captain, fitting the line that he had commanded a Solway trader, and Joseph was a farmer.

Richard Lawson

In the original canal survey report, Richard, of Drumburgh, was 'tide-surveyor of the Customs'.

In 1831, John Lawson of Bowness Hall names nephew Richard, a customs officer of Drumburgh, his executor and a major beneficiary.

William Chapman

Born 1749, died 1832

Although he wasn't a Cumbrian, Chapman merits a mention, as the engineer whose reports were the basis for the Carlisle canal.

He was born in Whitby, the eldest of ten children of Captain William Chapman and his second wife Hannah Baynes (there were three children from the first marriage).

The old jetty

Chapman junior became a mariner at 18, then a master mariner. He and brother John leased two collieries that went bankrupt in 1782, leading Chapman to turn to engineering.

He spent ten years in Ireland, where his unsolicited report proposing a canal south of Dublin brought him to the notice of the public.

During 1795 and 1796, he submitted several reports on the feasibility of building a canal from the river Tyne to Carlisle, and thence Maryport. This came to nothing.

He was appointed as engineer (1819) for the construction of the Carlisle Canal, but disputes with the directors saw him dismissed three months before it opened. In the book *A Biographical Dictionary of Civil Engineers in Great Britain and Ireland* (2002, Thomas Telford Publishing), his career spans nine pages, with a lengthy list of report, patents, and works.

Vessel	Type	Where, when built	Master	Owner(s)
Agnes	Sloop	Glencaple, 1826	John Sharp	The master
Alfred	Schooner	Wilton, 1815	Thomas Dalrymple	John Dixon & others
Ann	Sloop	Maryport, 1818	Robert Wood	The master
Ann and Mary	Smack	Salcombe, 1826	Thomas Radcliffe	**Peter Irving**
Ann and Mary	Sloop	Maryport, 1824	Adam Scott	Adam Scott
Archer	Barque	Ditto, 1830	John M'Matthewson	John Archer & others
Blenkinsop	Schooner	Carlisle, 1838	James Richardson	John Dixon & others
Britannia	Brig	W'haven, 1802	James Holliday	John Hewitt & others
Caledonia	Sloop	Kelton, 1815	James Scott	The master & M Beswick
Catherine	Sloop	Alloa, 1803	Peter Dickson	David Anderson
City of Carlisle	Steamer	Liverpool, 1834	**James Irving**	Carlisle, Annan & Liverpool Steam Co
Clarence	Steamer	D'barton, 1827	TA Maling	Carlisle Canal Company
Clio	Schooner	Maryport, 1837	William Geddes	Carlisle Canal Company
Crown	Sloop	Bowness, 1821	Jas Carruthers	The master & others
Dispatch	G	Carlisle, 1834	Francis Carruthers	Carlisle, Annan & Liverpool Steam Co
Doddington	Sloop	Northwich, 1830	John Watts	Carlisle & Liverpool Steam Company
Eden	Sloop	Annan, 1821	William Glover	John Wilson & others
Elizabeth	Schooner	Fowey, 1811	John Beattie	John Pickering
Friends	Schooner	Annan, 1837	John Baxter	William Bowman & others
Friendship	Wherry	Allonby, 1786	John Folder	Wm Graham & John Musgrave
Fortuna	Brig	Carlisle, 1827	Gideon Boyd	WR Martindale & others
Gamon	Galliot	Wilton, 1824	George Weild	Carlisle & Liverpool Steam Company
Hope	Schooner	Maryport, 1838	Thomas Brown	The Master
Industry	Wherry	Allonby, 1825	Jonathan Lowes	John Lowes
Isabella	Schooner	Prodsham, 1825	James Rome	**Peter Irving & others**
Jane	Brig	Carlisle, 1829	Tristram Rome	WR Martindale & others

List of Carlisle Vessels   1840   by William Sawyers

John	Fl	Northwich, 1802	John Irving	James Thompson
John	Sloop	Bowness, 1807	Joseph Thompson	Joseph Robinson
Mary	G	Garmouth, 1824	George Carruthers	Carlisle & Liverpool Steam Company
Mary	Schooner	Ulverston, 1827	David Irving	Peter Irving & others
Mary Ann Scott	Schooner	Maryport, 1831	William Gowan	Mark Thompson
Mary Appleby	Barque	Hampton, 1837	Thomas Mackie	David Anderson
Margaret	Sloop	Kelton, 1819	John Graves	The master
Miss Douglas	Schooner	Bowness, 1806	Hugh Davidson	William Black & others
Newcastle	Steamer	Birkenhead, 1834	Joseph Sewell	Carlisle & Liverpool Steam Company
Peace	Sloop	Wilton, 1814	John Scott	James Thomson
Phœbe	Sloop	Glencaple, 1826	Richard Irving	Margaret Irving & others
Prosperity	Sloop	Ditto, 1829	Thomas Bruster	William Black & others
Prosperity	Sloop	Ditto, 1779	Anthony Radcliff	Peter Irving
Rebecca	G	Garmouth, 1824	Joseph Shackley	Carlisle & Liverpool Steam Company
Rock	Sloop	Leftwich, 1806	Thomas Dixon	Carlisle, Annan & Liverpool Steam Co
Rosina	Sloop	W'haven, 1821	Anthony Glover	John Wilson & others
Royal Victoria	Steamer	Liverpool, 1837	John Hudson	Carlisle, Annan & Liverpool Steam Company
Shirleywich	Fl	Wilton, 1817	Jas Richardson	John Dixon & others
St Winifrid	G	Chester, 1816	John Smith	Carlisle, Annan & Liverpool Steam Co
Solway	Steamer	Holyhead, 1826	Thomas Burton	Carlisle & Liverpool Steam Company
Susan	Sloop	Wilton, 1804	Samuel Cheshire	James Thompson
Thomas	Schooner	Northwich, 1815	Robert Slater	Mark Thompson
Tryall	Sloop	Annan Water Foot, 1818	Jas Richardson	John Wilson & others
William & Nancy	Sloop	Kelton, 1817	William Musgrave	The master

3

The wet dock that never was

IN SAMUEL Jefferson's 1838 *History and Antiquities of Carlisle*, the Port is described as 'the place where vessels of more than 100 tons burden discharge their cargoes'.

The book says that 44 vessels then belonged to the Port.

Until 1826, it was just sailing vessels. No Steam Packets before then, it would seem! By spring 1844, there were four of them (steam packets).

The book also mentions that an Act of Parliament has been made to construct a 'wet' dock, 'which it is expected will shortly be carried into execution'.

TIDAL BASIN, PORT CARLISLE

An old postcard

Of utmost importance

As I mentioned in the main canal chapter, the idea of the new dock was to enable steam ships to dock there even at low tide.

In 1835, Peter Dixon, chairman of the Carlisle and Liverpool Steam Navigation Company, wrote to the canal company. His letter says the floating dock 'is of utmost importance to the convenience and safety of vessels resorting to the canal, particularly steam vessels and others of large burthen'.

The steam company hoped the dock would be built as soon as possible, being fully persuaded that the additional tonnage rates which would be paid for such accommodation would be counter-balanced by the additional security and convenience offered, and would eventually produce an adequate return for the capital expended.

It was certainly gone into at great length. The first references to it in the local press can be found in 1833, when the *Carlisle Journal* thought the rapidly increasing trade of Carlisle made a wet dock 'highly desirable – if not absolutely necessary'.

The Journal trusted no time would be lost in bringing it to fruition.

Two years later, the canal company committee visited the Port to examine the proposed site of the new dock. They were accompanied by Sir James Graham, Admiral Malcolm, William Blamire MP, William Marshall MP, Phillip Howard MP, and Henry Aglionby MP.

A meeting was held in Carlisle Town Hall soon after, to empower the committee to start the proceedings needed to secure the Act of Parliament.

'A second Liverpool'

Hopes being ever-high, it was suggested a wet dock was all Port Carlisle needed to become 'a second Liverpool' – able to trade directly with ports around the globe.

The Notice of Intent (to seek an Act of Parliament) was posted in November 1835.

It didn't go down well in west Cumberland, where they were looking for backing to build railway lines from Carlisle to Maryport and to Whitehaven. Their objections might not have greatly mattered – and Maryport and Whitehaven didn't see eye to eye on things their end (as both the Carlisle Journal and the Carlisle Patriot pointed out).

However, the opinion of one pro-west-coast figure DID matter. Because the canal company needed to get Lord Lonsdale onside. The Lowthers had owned the Barony of Burgh since the 1600s, including the beach where the dock would be built.

And selling Port Carlisle as a 'new Liverpool' probably wasn't going to cut it with someone whose family had transformed Whitehaven from a fishing village to a major port.

His lordship does seem to have got sniffy about agreeing to the dock, citing manorial rights and enjoyment of the space.

William Nanson, the canal company secretary, wrote to Lord Lonsdale in August 1836, reminding him that he already received an anchorage payment for each vessel. 'A trifling amount,' but he still got more from one steam vessel in a year than he had in total annual receipts before the canal was built.

William pointed out his lordship could also build warehouses if he wished.

The emphasis of the letter was that Lord L would benefit financially from the dock, but wouldn't make a penny from the beach if he didn't.

Another part-letter (missing who it was from, possibly his agent) advises Lord L he can effectively name his price.

The canal company might be trying to convince him the land was of little value. But (the writer points out), it was of great value to the canal company as without it, they wouldn't be able to maintain the jetty, quays or buildings already built.

The ink was barely dry

Sir James Graham presented a petition to the House of Commons in February 1836, asking the house to grant the required Act. It duly went through the Commons and Lord, receiving royal assent on June 7.

But doubt was already more than creeping in. The canal committee reported a month later that it had asked Mr Hartley, the engineer, to 'reconsider and determine upon the most eligible mode of executing the works'. His advice was to (initially) just build the outer dock, which should provide ample accommodation for some time.

The annual report of 1838 says the steam berth has been enlarged; extra accommodation has been made for loading/unloading vessels too big to enter the canal, and; the cut from the low-water channel had been widened.

'Your committee have reason to expect that a convenient tide dock may be constructed at a comparatively moderate expense'.

Tenders were sought that summer for the excavation of about 30,000 yards of the beach, the creation of an embankment, and facing it with masonry. It says this was to enlarge the dock (not create a wet/floating/tide dock).

In December, the Journal reported that 'active preparations' for the new wet and dry docks had been going on for some time, and a pier was to be built as soon as the weather permitted.

'I know what the canal needs'

And, er, that was that. Until December 1845, when (as mentioned in the main canal chapter) someone signing themselves Huna wrote to the *Carlisle Journal* with a bright idea.

The open letter to the canal committee started 'your canal wants improving'. The suggestion was that the company should build a sea lock, deepen the basin at Port Carlisle, enlarge it to take more vessels, and extend the canal from the basin to the sea lock by a cut.

No one seems to have publicly asked: 'why haven't you built the wet dock yet?' The letter is as close as

it gets in a way, in that it may have prompted readers to wonder 'whatever happened to..?'

The question was answered – in 1855. A passage outlining the background to the Silloth Bay project says the Port's harbour was inadequate, but by the time the new dock got the go-ahead, circumstances were changing. The railway system was growing, trade was changing considerably, and it 'became questionable how far it was politic' to build the wet dock.

The canal had 'struggled on,' but from 1841, 'it became obvious that it was useless' to bother building the dock.

By then, the canal was struggling financially, and the port had been affected by sand (thanks to Raven Bank Jetty). It would only be a couple of years before attention turned to converting the canal to a railway.

And the only wet dock anyone would be interested in building would be at Silloth.

Footnote

In October 1853, when the canal had been drained and was being turned into a railway, a letter appeared in the Patriot.

It is addressed to the Silloth Bay Railway and Dock Company, and says its author has been asked on its behalf to report on the most desirable plan for construction a floating dock at Silloth Bay.

John Bernard Hartley was a civil engineer who had worked on docks (and lighthouses) across the UK. He had been been asked for his views on providing dock accommodation at Port Carlisle, and had visited both places on September 23.

His conclusion was that as long as any works at the Port could be affected by works carried out by other Solway land proprietors, it would not be wise shelling out on a floating dock.

In 1835, when the dock was first proposed, there was a distinct and definable channel running up to and past Port Carlisle, which vessels could use with ease and certainty.

However, 'some pier or jetty work above the Port' had altered the course of the river Eden.

At Port Carlisle now, in front of the entrance to the quay, off the end of the jetty, there was a high and extensive bank of sand, forming a barrier to all approach other than at fully high water. Meanwhile, the only channel now was a narrow, tortuous gutter, turning sharp round the jetty end, and running along the land.

The cost of remedial work would be considerable – and pointless, as long as other land owners controlled works above the Port.

As for the agitators the canal company had used to try to solve the sand problem, in November 1853, they were said (by a letter-writer called Civis) to be peeping out of a mud bank which had half-buried them.

And during the hearings into the Silloth Bay Railway and Dock Bill, in 1855, engineers for that project concurred it would be 'imprudent' to spend money at Port Carlisle.

Peter Irving was still using the Port for his medium-sized vessels, and would continue to do so until for sure the mid 1860s, possibly until his death in 1869. But he was pretty much the only real user.

Back in 1855, Mr Hartley, civil engineer to the Liverpool Dock Trust, opined that Port Carlisle 'was done for'.

4

The railway

The remains of the platform can still be seen

BEFORE writing about the railway, it is important to emphasise that there was – obviously – a gap between the canal closing and the railway being ready to operate.

During that gap, importers/exporters/holidaymakers/travellers/residents/everyone either had to find an alternative means of transport to get to/from Port Carlisle. Or not bother, and find a port/resort that they could get to.

Some of that traffic went to Maryport, who weren't keen to lose it back!

One enterprising person did come up with something to fill the gap.

Early in August 1853, the *Carlisle Patriot* observed that while the water had yet to be drained from the canal, the question (of the gap) had already arisen. However, a Mr John C—— (the page is too faint to read; it looks like 'Cowx') had 'very spiritedly' undertaken to run an omnibus between the city and the port every day except Monday.

The Patriot thought he deserved support from travellers, saying those accustomed to making the journey could now do so in an omnibus rather than an aquabus.

The short version

The railway in a nutshell is this: the canal was closed in the summer of 1853, and drained. Rails were laid either on the old bed or alongside. The aim was to form a continuous rail line from Newcastle to Port Carlisle (the original idea of the canal was for a continuous canal from Newcastle to Port Carlisle). It cost just £2,793 a mile to build, and opened to passenger traffic on June 22, 1854.

But within two years, it had been downgraded to a branch line, because Port Carlisle was being superseded in all respects by Silloth.

Its history from circa 1856 on is covered in the chapters on Silloth, and on the Dandy.

Which doesn't leave a lot to cover here!

A muted affair

It didn't get a great deal of coverage at the time, to be honest.

The line opened on February 8, 1854. The event received 14 lines in the Patriot that Saturday.

The 17th annual report of the Carlisle Total Abstinence Society got 23 lines.

The Patriot did report there was 'great rejoicing' at Port Carlisle at the arrival of the first locomotive. And thought that when fully open, the line would be a boon to the public at both ends.

The rest of the report, however, was praise of the contractor (a Mr Simpson), for overcoming difficulties such as bad weather and the fact the

bottom of the canal hadn't proved ideal for rail tracks in places.

That was it. No half-day in Carlisle, no bands, no fanfares, no grand speeches (there probably were speeches, but the local press wasn't interested enough to report any of it).

It was nice for residents of the village, but beyond that, no big deal.

Better than the alternative

It hadn't even been universally popular from the start. After all, the idea of turning the canal into a railway had been borne more of desperation than conviction that a railway would make everyone their fortune.

In December 1852, canal shareholder George Saul was anything but pleased. He held shares in his own right and on behalf of others, and thought the idea monstrous. Primarily because he thought it should have required the unanimous consent of all shareholders, bond holders and creditors.

George said it was irrelevant that the canal was unprofitable – if that was all it took for a company to be treated this way, half the businesses in the country could be handed over to others who thought they could run them better.

George called the railway 'pure speculation,' the spending of any canal company money in connection with it as 'misapplication of funds', and said he was determined to oppose this 'spoilation' of canal property.

His may have been a rare voice among those with money invested in the canal – most people accepted the railway at least as a less-bad bet than the canal.

But he wasn't the only one gloomy about the railway's prospects.

A Looker-On, in a letter to the Patriot in February 1853, said the supposed advantages of a Port Carlisle railway required leaping to conclusions, and speculation.

If there was a great potential, in terms of coal/coke/salts/alkalis from Newcastle, how come the Tyneside producers weren't already using the existing west Cumberland railways, to the coastal ports?

The old platform

Another letter by A Looker On, a few weeks later, has some thinly veiled references to key figures in the proceedings: "Peter the Great, at the head of a large manufacturing firm in this city, has for some years past had Dusty Miller under his personal care, preparing him to appear in public as propounder and advocate of the Carlisle Canal Conversion Scheme."

Peter the Great is clearly Peter Dixon. Dusty Miller must mean Jonathan Dodgson Carr, founder of the biscuit company.

A Looker On again casts doubts on the ability of a railway to attract business – other than that of the Carlisle manufacturers who, he says, only want a railway for their own benefit.

The writer says if they want a railway, they should build their own, not expect the public to pay for one.

This may have been unfair on Dixon and Carr, but realistically, why else would manufacturers want to build a railway unless it was of benefit to them?

A whining petition

Whether A Looker On was simply a Maryport railway shareholder, we can only guess. For sure, the idea didn't go down well there.

The Maryport and Carlisle Railway Company went so far as to present a petition (to the House of Commons) against it. William Halton publicly called this 'a whining, pitiful petition' that was 'more like a child crying lest the rattle should be taken from it than anything else'. While Joseph Rome asked, rhetorically, if it truly was a case of converting a useful canal into a useless railway (as opponents said), then what were these opponents afraid of?!

And G Sibson also took Maryport to task for saying its railway well supplied the needs of the district – pointing out that line didn't serve the needs of the villages between Carlisle and the Port.

A public meeting was held in Carlisle to start a counter-petition in favour. This was signed by 'a large majority of the most respectable and influential habitants' of the city.

A follow-up meeting was covered in great detail by the Patriot (in April 1853). But the first speaker, John Hewson, was telling in his words. And the whole affair comes over as far less hopeful and optimistic than previously.

John Hewson did say the railway would be of immense advantage to the city and the public. And there were speakers who talked up Port Carlisle as a port. But he also said it was the only chance for those with investments in the canal company to get any money back.

And alderman John Irving also made it clear if they didn't approve a railway, the canal would very likely have to close anyway.

Sidelined before a sleeper was laid

William Halton once said publicly that the canal had made Carlisle prosperous.

In fact, while that 'favour' had to some extent been two-ended, the people whose voices mattered were all at the city end. As early as August 1853 – just a few weeks after the canal had shut and six months before the Port Carlisle Railway opened – it was being claimed its supporters had started to look literally beyond the Port.

William Geddes, superintendent of lights and buoys on the Solway, had previously been a champion of its navigational possibilities.

However, at a civic fish dinner in Port Carlisle in August 1853, it was claimed a letter had been read out from him saying: "Nature seems against us ever having a good harbour at Port Carlisle, it being too far up the Frith to command deep water and a clear entrance; but in my opinion, Silloth might be made the best harbour in Cumberland."

Even Peter Irving, who had been such a champion of the Port, who lived there, and charged and discharged his ships there, seems to have bowed down to practicality. For sure, by 1855, he was giving evidence in favour of the Silloth Bay project, extolling its advantages and saying as long as there was a deep channel, it didn't matter where it was.

Back in August 1853, 'Master Mariner' of Maryport popped up in the Patriot to say: "I told you so."

He also says the entrance to the harbour at Port Carlisle is sanded up (*see the section on the dock that never was*). And says a good and useful canal is being destroyed to make way for an expensive and useless railway.

Master Mariner reminds readers of the claims a railway would make Port Carlisle another Liverpool, and of the hope of the canal company investors that it would enable to them to get some of their money back. Saying this hope now seems vain, he add: "No sooner is the Act passed than the expectant proprietors are again told that all this anticipated greatness was mere moonshine."

The despotic and the cheated

In December 1853, two letter writers to the Patriot criticised the Silloth plan, with one summing up the situation of the now-competing interests of Silloth and Port Carlisle.

'Scrutator' likened the situation to the 'despotic' Russian czar, cheating the oppressed Danubian principalities while pretending concern for them.

Scrutator says the Silloth promoters have likewise been flattering the Port Carlisle Railway Company with professions of friendship, when all they really want is access to the Carlisle to Drumburgh stretch of the PCR. He points out that for the Silloth Bay dock to succeed, the Port must fail. And the fact that some of the Silloth company are also PC company members does not mean the interests of the two companies align.

He says there are three ways forward.

1. One is for the Silloth company to totally take control of the nine-mile Carlisle to Drumburgh stretch of the PC line.

2. Two is for the two companies to share profits equally.

3. Three is for them to work independently and compete for traffic, with the PCR charging Silloth for using the nine-mile stretch.

One would make the PC company worthless; two would probably mean neither could pay dividends; three would show for sure that the interests of the two companies did clash.

Scrutator's advice? He points out that those who have investment in the PCR are stuck with it – they'd just have to make the best of it.

The theme is hope, right?

He does, however, hold out a ray of hope for them, though it is hardly the sunny optimism expressed by others in this book:

"If they hold their own, it may yet prove not so bad."

The protagonists

The Port Carlisle Railway Company was effectively the canal company reborn. The initial directors were: William James, William Marshall, John Dixon, George Dixon (all covered in the canal chapter), along with Rev John Heysham, and Jonathan Dodgson Carr. John Nanson was secretary.

Jonathan Carr (1806-1884) needs little introduction beyond what I've already said: he was the founder of the biscuit company. The factory is still emitting enticing odours today, under the umbrella of United Biscuits. JD started his bakery business in Carlisle in 1831, after walking there from his home in Kendal.

He moved it to Caldewgate in 1837 – handy for the canal.

Reverend John Heysham
Born circa 1793. Died 1877

The only Reverend John Heysham I can find is the son of Dr John Heysham, who is principally remembered for the meticulous (and valuable) statistics he kept on diseases and deaths in Carlisle. Rev John's brother Thomas was a prominent naturalist, magistrate, and mayor in Carlisle.

John, was vicar of Lazonby for the last 30 years of his life. He was also a magistrate. He didn't marry.

George Sibson

The man who in 1853 spoke up for villagers at first had me thinking of a Port Carlisle family. There were Sibsons at Westfield House in 1881. They'd be interested in a railway link to Carlisle.

In 1851, the only George Sibson of a suitable age was a solicitor, living in Fisher Street with his wife Jane, four young children, and two domestics.

This George was born about 1809. He'd retired to Grinsdale by 1861, dying there in 1874. It was presumably Grinsdale he was thinking of in his comments about the villages needing a rail link. However, he was also inadvertently speaking up on behalf of his family a few decades later.

Because with George and Jane in 1851 is Thomas, aged eight... who is the farmer I was thinking of at Westfield House in 1881 and 1891.

William Geddes
Born circa 1811, died 1879

William Geddes was superintendent of lights and buoys, and sub-commissioner of pilotage under the

Trinity Board. He'd known the Solway since 1834, his father having been there before him. He was employed in laying down buoys in the channel for the shipowners of Carlisle and assisted in a survey of the Solway in 1851. Born in Scotland, he was living that year in Skinburness, with his wife Mary, daughter Mary Ann, and a domestic.

They were at Skinburness in 1841, William described then as a mariner. On the same page were a William Geddes, mariner, aged 60, Mary 63, and George, 38, mariner – also all born Scotland.

In 1871, William, Mary and Mary Ann were living at North House, Silloth. He died at Silloth in 1879.

Thomas Geddes
Born circa 1780

Thomas Geddes was keeper of the Lee Scar Lighthouse, formerly a mariner, and had known the Solway since about 1805.

He was born in Dumfries around 1780. In 1861, aged 84 and married (but, understandably on his own), he was recorded on the census as residing at Silloth lighthouse.

John Hewson
Born circa 1792, died 1856

John Hewson was a Carlisle cotton manufacturer. In 1851-52, he was also the mayor of Carlisle. At that time, he was living in Fisher Street, with his wife Margaret, her widowed mother Isabella Hodgson, and two domestics. In 1848, he was a land tax commissioner for Carlisle. And his name shows up in a petition to the House of Lords in 1852 about a matter relating to the North of England Joint Stock Banking Company.

John Irving

Born circa 1813

John Irving was described by one letter-writer as 'for political purposes, the right arm of the right hon Sir James Graham' (Whig politician, and MP for Carlisle, for the second time from 1852-1861).

An alderman and a businessman, in 1855 John Irving said he was a guano and seed merchant, who had been in business upwards of 17 years. The 1851 census gives even more detail: he had apparently told the enumerator he was an alderman, grocer, tallow chandler, and seed merchant, occupier of 34 acres and joint occupier of 100 acres of land. Didn't mention the guano at that point!

He, his wife Ann, four children, two domestics and two apprentices took up so much space on the census form, the enumerator didn't bother to the page for any other household.

The Irvings were living at 61 Ferguson Lane. Ten years later, they were at St Nicholas Place, London Road, there were ten children and four domestics. John gave his place of birth as either Arthuret or Longtown. And despite one letter-writer wondering, there was no connection with Peter of Port Carlisle.

George Saul
Born circa 1796

George Saul was a Carlisle solicitor, who created the Brunstock House estate in the late 1820s, building a mansion and laying out a park. His legal firm was founded by his father Silas, whose memorial can be seen in Carlisle cathedral. George and John Dixon of Knells were among the chief subscribers to the building of Houghton church and school, built in 1841.

In 1851, he and wife Luna (née Fearon) were at Brunstock, with a cook, a housemaid, and a butler.

5

Silloth, the new port of Carlisle

The city manufacturers wanted a local port. When Port Carlisle proved problematic, they looked elsewhere

IN 1855, Sir James Graham, MP for Carlisle, dug the first sod of the Silloth Railway at Drumburgh. It certainly wasn't the first nail in the coffin for Port Carlisle's commercial prosperity, but it was a nail.

For when completed – the first trains ran on August 28, 1856 – it meant people (and goods) could travel from Carlisle to Silloth without troubling the Port. And Drumburgh to Port Carlisle was reduced to being a branch line: a 'no-through road.

Which wouldn't have mattered if the Port had continued to welcome cargo ships and passenger steamers. But of course, it didn't.

Port Carlisle 'in a good state'

An account of the Port Carlisle Dock and Railway company's annual meeting, on July 31, 1856, says the receipts for the year to May 31 were £3,699, about £909 up on the previous year.

There's no mention of the interest payments they had to find. But, the chairman did (without figures) refer to unexpected outlays due to a shed fire, and flooding (by the sea) of the line. And the cost of lighting and buoying the channel remained 'onerous'.

The directors reported that the Carlisle to Silloth Bay Railway from Drumburgh to Silloth would soon open, and would work in connection with the Port Carlisle

A trip to Silloth in the 1930s, from an old family album

line (they shared the first eight-and-half miles).

Ever the optimists, they also reported that the harbour at Port Carlisle was in a good state and the number of vessels using it had risen. This had been helped by turning part of the old canal into a reservoir, which had had the effect of scouring the harbour, at very little expense.

The chairman, William James of Barrock Park, admitted there was no marked improvement in the company's financial provision, but said their prospects were brighter than the previous year. Their passenger traffic was steadily and gradually improving, as was merchandise traffic – although that was still far too limited.

32

As he'd said 'on more than one occasion', trade lost is hard to recover, and rarely done rapidly. They'd lost trade between the closure of the canal and the completion of the railway, but progress since was in the right direction.

A fine new screw-steamer had now been bought and placed on the station which he hoped would be the start of a new era of prosperity for the company.

However, they were in a state of transition, like a chrysalis and only when the landing bay and dock at Silloth were completed would they truly find their wings.

Or was it all hope and hype again?

For sure, the Port is mentioned often in Shipping Intelligence, including Peter Irving's Peace, regularly carrying coals to Annan and returning with ballast (for the new railway?). And Peter's brig Robert Burns was still sailing from the Port to Quebec.

A 'for sale' notice in 1857 for a 72-foot-long schooner, the Rapid, gives her dimensions: breadth, 17ft 10; depth, 11ft 10; draws 12 feet of water, with 215 tons of cargo dead weight. She was lying at Port Carlisle, having just discharged a cargo of Indian corn 'from Galatz'. (When the Rapid put in a Maryport on New Year's Day 1858, on her way to Dublin, the port tried to charge her harbour dues. The captain refused, as he'd only put in due to bad weather – exempting him from dues. The port trustees then seized the Rapid's anchor in lieu of payment!).

However, a report in June 1856 about the 'fine new screw-steamer' (set to operate from Port Carlisle to Liverpool twice a week) was clear that this was only until the Silloth railway line was open. The new vessel was called Silloth.

The Carlisle Patriot seemed to take pleasure a month later in reporting problems that had beset the (ship) Silloth, problems that had hit the Silloth railway – and the fact that the Robert Burns had anchored in Catherine Hole, near Silloth and was transporting her cargo to Port Carlisle by raft, 'it not being deemed safe to venture further'.

The Patriot had a somewhat sly and sarcastic dig: 'why she did not go up we know not, unless it was for want of water, though it has been repeatedly said there is no want of water at Port Carlisle.'

The paper says the brig would have done far better to use Maryport, before mentioning another vessel anchoring in Catherine Hole: 'so much for cheap and expeditious navigation in the Solway'.

Some painful sums

The Patriot also followed up the AGM (on August 9, 1856) with a report 'from a correspondent,' about the financial affairs of the Port Carlisle Dock and Railway company.

It lists a bunch of figures, including the liabilities of the canal company, summing it up as: 'this analysis makes the company debtor on capital account £17,453 15s 9d, in addition to the old debt of £84,536 1s 3d which was the canal's legacy.

The article reminds readers the revenue balance (which it puts at £873, rather than £909) has to meet the interest on mortgage loans, bankers' balances, preference stock, etc. It puts the bill for those payments at just over £3,265. The only way to meet the payments would be to borrow more – increasing the debt and the interest due.

The author, who thinks the banks will soon 'stop the tap', calls the situation lamentable and says the shareholders must be sick at the non-realisation of the promises held out to them. He also forewarns that if the company amalgamates with the Silloth company that it 'is in no better pecuniary position'.

In fact, at the Silloth company's AGM, in September 1856, Mr James said both companies were in the same boat and must sink or swim together. The Port Carlisle railway could scarcely keep its head above water and looked on the Silloth company as a drowning man looked on a life jacket.

Mixing his metaphors, he added the Port Carlisle Railway directors hoped the Silloth company would help a lame dog over the stile.

By then, the steamer the Silloth had switched to its eponymous new port.

Singing in (spite of) the rain

August 28, 1856 was a wet Thursday – it rained heavily and incessantly. But there was still a buzz in Carlisle (helped by the mayor recommending the shops shut for the occasion).

A band and banners saw off the first train, which was so full a second had to be provided.

The *Carlisle Journal* reported that the passengers became very excited in the approaches to Port Carlisle – but it was not on the Port's account. It was because from Drumburgh, they were on the new line, which took them to a

refreshment marquee, the beach, and – finally – some sunshine, at Silloth.

There was the usual dinner for dignitaries, two of whom sang (respectively) a verse of a Cumbrian ballad and 'The last new sheun our Betty gat'.

There were lots of speeches, toasts – and songs.

From then on, the train timetables had to advise passengers (from Carlisle): 'Port Carlisle passengers change carriages at Drumburgh.'

'The new port of Carlisle'

On August 18, 1857, there were crowds and fanfares once more, and a general holiday in Carlisle. Sadly for Port Carlisle, the cheers were for the laying of the foundation stone of the new dock at Silloth.

The *Carlisle Patriot*, reporting on the event a few days later, informed anyone who didn't already know that the new dock would supplant that at Port Carlisle, 'which has long been almost useless in consequence of the silting up of the sand.'

Silloth would 'become the new port of Carlisle'.

The Patriot predicted that within a few years, readers could expect to see a flourishing town where

---

PORT CARLISLE RAILWAY.

OPENING OF THE CARLISLE AND SILLOTH BAY RAILWAY,

ON THURSDAY, 28th OF AUGUST.

TRAINS will LEAVE CARLISLE at 12 o'Clock, calling at Burgh only. A TRAIN will LEAVE DRUMBURGH at 2 o'Clock, calling at Kirkbride and the Abbey, RETURNING from SILLOTH p.m., calling at the Abbey, Kirkbride, Drumburgh, and Burgh. RETURN TICKETS ls. Each; to be obtained at the Port Carlisle Stations, or at 48, Castle Street. CARLISLE.

N.B.—No Tickets will be issued after 6 o'Clock on Wednesday Evening, the 27th instant.

By Order. _____ A PIXTON, Manager.
Aug. 21st, 1856.

A PUBLIC DINNER will be provided by Mr. Harding, in a TENT adjoining the Solway Hotel, at Silloth. P. J. Dixon, Esq, Chairman the Company, in the Chair. —

Tickets 3s. Each, to be had at 48, Castle Street; and at the Port Carlisle Stations; and from Mr. HARDING, Silloth.

until the preparatory works started there had only been 'an extensive rabbit warren.'

The day began with bands playing in Carlisle, before several thousand citizens boarded special trains, pulled by engines decorated with flags and evergreens. Cannons and martial music provided a salute to send them on their way.

Meanwhile, Sir James Graham, MP for Carlisle, and a long list of civic and railway dignitaries enjoyed a lunch laid on by the mayor, George Mounsey, before boarding a special train for Silloth. Where Sir James did the honours with a trowel. A silver one, befitting the occasion.

Before the foundation stone was fixed fully, a time-capsule box was put into it, containing coins of the realm, copies of the three Carlisle papers, charts and plans.

When it came to the after-dinner speeches later, Sir James said it was "only necessary for any person who was present when the first sod of the Silloth Railway was turned, two years ago, to pass over the line now, to look at the buildings erected, the jetty where a steamer from Liverpool was unloading – one of the swiftest going out of the Mersey in the coasting trade – to see the works in progress.... and form a confident opinion that this undertaking will not fail."

He also spoke about the safety of the Solway for shipping, adding: "when the works here are completed, the most dangerous part, the narrowest part – between Silloth and Port Carlisle – will no longer be traversed."

What folk in Port Carlisle thought of all this can only be imagined. Did they regard it as inevitable, or think the bands and flags (if they even knew about them) were rubbing salt into a wound?

There were crumbs of comfort offered. A toast was offered to the directors of the Port Carlisle Railway – for at first realising the canal was doomed and proposing to turn it into a railway, and for then backing the Silloth Railway and dock plans. Why, if Silloth prospered, they might even get to pay a dividend one day to their shareholders (laughter).

Over to someone else

Silloth dock opened on August 3, 1857 – again, shops shut at 10am, there were bands in the streets of the city and special trains were laid on from Carlisle for anyone wanting to witness the occasion. In fact, there weren't enough trains to meet demand – something like 10,000 people had decided to take part in the occasion.

There is a story to be told about how things turned out for Silloth – its railway company, its port. in fact, by 1860, the Silloth Bay Railway and Company's annual accounts statement makes grim reading: expenditure, £13,380; income £3,014.

The railway and dock had cost, all costs included, more than £300,000 to build, and almost £12,000 of the annual expenditure was interest payments.

There is plenty to be told, of course, about the whole Silloth project from its inception. For instance, Lord Lonsdale was very much an opponent, writing in 1833 to his agent/secretary: "I am rather in doubt as to the proper thing to do in opposing the Silloth Bay Project.

"I don't like to have anything to do with the railway company, for somehow or another, you always have the want of it."

But, this is a book about Port Carlisle, so I'm only mentioning other places as and when they impacted on the Port.

6

Cut off entirely

The viaduct whose remains can still be seen jutting into the Solway was the final straw for the Port

The English side today

What the Port Carlisle railway had that others wanted was access to Carlisle, and a city station.

What no one much was interested in by the time the railway opened in 1854 was access to the Port.

And as the money men and developers of both the canal and the railway had always been city manufacturers and city politicians, their loyalty to Port Carlisle was pretty thin.

They needed access to/from the sea: where was a matter of practicality and cost – after all, it was only for those reasons that an otherwise obscure spot called Fisher's Cross had been chosen in the first place.

Once the manufacturers decided to focus on Silloth, they lost interest in and neglected Port Carlisle.

Had nothing else happened to further damage the Port, it's unlikely history would have been any different. The harbour had a sand problem it would have taken great expense to resolve. Which made Silloth look a better bet. The harbour was tidal, which also made Silloth look a better bet.

So perhaps in the overall scheme of things, the viaduct didn't make a great deal of difference.

That isn't to say it did no harm.

But first, a little rewind

The idea of viaduct wasn't new. Someone came up with the idea of a bridge from Bowness to Annan in 1830, in an anonymous pamphlet, *Remarks on the Utility and Practicability of the Formation of a Rail Road between Whitehaven and Carlisle.*

It was met with scorn. The *Cumberland Pacquet and Ware's Advertiser* called the idea sublime, utopian, stupendous and bordering on certain of the Munchausen achievements. Likening it to the idea of a bridge from Scotland to Ireland, the paper suggested the engineer move it down to the Robin Rigg sandbank, so vessels running aground there could shelter beneath it.

And in 1836, the idea popped up again, under the pointed headline: 'Another railway from Preston to Glasgow!' The *Kendal Mercury* this time reported on (another) plan to build a £3million railway between those two places, saying it deserved praise for boldness, if not for feasibility. It would include a ten-mile 'embankment' over Morecambe Bay, and a viaduct over the Solway from Port Carlisle.

The paper assured readers that it wasn't hoaxing them, calling it 'one of the wildest speculations of the present speculation period'.

Do not pass Go, do not collect £200...

Indeed, in the middle of the 19th century, it seemed like everyone wanted to build railways. In all directions, and via anywhere and everywhere.

In 1858, for example, the Caledonian Railway Company wanted to make a branch railway to the Port Carlisle Railway. A draft Bill was before Parliament. Another proposed line – the North British – had been thrown out.

The PCR and Silloth railway companies were meanwhile opposing the proposed Langholm line, which the Caledonian had a huge interest in. The Langholm line was a rival project to the Liddesdale scheme. Both were intended to create a railway between Hawick and Carlisle.

We are still talking 1858. The battle to build a line connecting Carlisle to Hawick had been dragging on since 1845.

It get a mention in this book because the Port Carlisle Railway company hoped it would connect with their line.

In the end it did, with the NBR negotiating a lease with the PCR (and Silloth railway), to gain access to the Carlisle station. The NBR was to rescue the PCR from its financial problems (*see the chapter on the Dandy*).

Getting straight to the point

The promoters of the Dumfriesshire and Cumberland (Solway Junction) Railway Bill of 1862 wanted a short cut to take iron ore from Cumbrian mines to Lanarkshire's furnaces, without having to go through Carlisle. They were carrying more than 100,000 tons of the stuff a year to Scotland from west Cumberland at that time.

The chosen route ran from Brayton to Kirtlebridge – and right across the Solway from a point a short walk west of Bowness. This would save 14 miles and 22 miles on the two old routes that were being used.

Plan A was to construct embankments, a viaduct and OPENING BRIDGE, similar to that at Leven Sands, Morecambe Bay. This would house a 36 ft 'drawbridge', 'so simple in construction it can be worked by a man and a boy'.

Like other railways, it involved protracted debate and negotiations. And one person who went all the way down to London to have his say was Port Carlisle ship owner Peter Irving.

A bridge too far down

In June 1864, Peter was invited to give evidence to a House of Lords select committee, having petitioned against the viaduct.

A month earlier, Sir James Brunlees, the viaduct's architect, told a House of Commons committee that in his experience from Morecambe Bay, the structure would IMPROVE navigation on the Solway.

The Board of Trade was worried that the solid embankments would cause 'a serious stagnation of the tidal stream' with the result that there would be 'an acceleration of deposit both below and above the interference, and a proportional exclusion of tidal influence'.

Brunlees reckoned that at Morecambe, the channels in the Kent and Leven had deepened (by eight and two feet respectively).

He also rejected the fear that that the viaduct piers would mean the tidal stream was forced through them with greatly increased velocity, but with a reduced effect on maintaining the depth of the channel.

And he reckoned vessels of up to 120 tons were able to pass through the 36 feet gaps at Morecambe Bay just fine – there had been no complaints.

It's interesting that he put the number of vessels sailing up the Solway to the Port (not counting ships crossing from the Port to Annan) as around 80 a year. That's well down from the 1830s, when it was more like 365.

The same parliamentary hearing was also told it may be worthwhile connecting the new line with the main Port Carlisle/Silloth line. But there was no point at all linking the new railway with the Port Carlisle branch line – there was no traffic to/from Port Carlisle to make it worthwhile.

Mind the gaps

In June 1864, Peter told the house he was the owner of several vessels: one of 650 tons, others of 260, 90, 80 and so on. He did a considerable trade shipping coals, slate, manure etc.

He said Port Carlisle was a very good dock for medium-sized vessels. There was an awkward bank there at present, but the sand had been worse before and had got better again.

Peter said the width of beam of some of his vessels varied from 16 feet to 32 – and the bridge spans were proposed to be 36 feet wide. It would be dangerous in certain states of the tide and wind for vessels to get through the bridge, and it would seriously harm the shipping trade.

He did admit his large vessels had not visited the Port since 1862, and 'did not pretend that Port Carlisle was a good harbour for large vessels' – because it was not a wet dock. But, it was as good a dry dock as any in the kingdom.

If Port Carlisle was shut up, it would cost him £135 a year more in port dues. He would also lose a large proportion of his coal trade.

The Port dismissed as worthless

Peter's wasn't quite a lone voice in defence of the Port. For one thing, eleven people (mostly residents) signed a petition to Parliament. One source says this claimed the viaduct would reduce the value of their properties. Another says it claimed the viaduct would interfere with access to their harbour. In fact, it was both, as the petition was got up by owners of warehouses and port shareholders.

At the June 1864 House of Lords hearing, the promoters of the railway first tried to claim the Port Carlisle petitioners had no right to be heard.

When the committee decided otherwise, the witness said Port Carlisle was port in name only, and would be improved by the railway.

This Mr Mundell also said many of the village's houses were empty, and no doubt many more would be so soon. The channel was filling up and trade was trifling.

The Morecambe bridge master, William Smith, said he often had half-a-dozen vessels though his bridge and back again in half an hour. He'd been to Port Carlisle, there were only a couple of small vessels, and it didn't seem like a port to him.

It was nothing but a sandbank.

It wasn't just 'outsiders'. F Warring, collector of customs at Carlisle and the Port, said there had been no foreign trade there since 1862 – it all now went to Silloth. The customs house office had likewise been moved there.

Thomas Asbridge, of Drumburgh, who had been 'intimate' with the Solway and its channels for more than 50 years, also thought the viaduct would improve navigation.He also spoke about properties at the Port being empty, and said the harbour was effectively silted up. He'd known Port Carlisle quite as bad as it was now and yet recover. He thought the bridge would help this.

And W Wood, pilot of Port Carlisle, thought an opening of 36 feet in the bridge would be safe for vessels to pass through – before admitting he should not care very much to try it himself!

The Port's other champions

James Hastie, master mariner, Port Carlisle, also gave evidence to the Lords in June 1864, saying the bridge as proposed would cause great inconvenience, if not danger, to vessels navigating the Solway. He had tried to get a vessel through where the 36 ft opening would be, and found he could not do so with safety, except under very favourable circumstances. The bridge would interfere with the shipping between the Port and Annan.

There was also Joseph Ferguson.

The August 1864 half-yearly meeting of the Port Carlisle Dock and Railway Company could been held in a garden shed rather than the company office. Only W B Page (who presided) and John Nanson, the secretary, turned up.

The PRC had by then leased everything to the NBR, of course, so meetings probably did seem a waste of time to most shareholders. They did at least get a £1 10s per cent, per annum dividend out of it.

However, there was one point of interest: a letter from Joseph Ferguson, asking the committee to explain why they hadn't opposed, in Parliament, the crossing over the frith by the Solway Junction Railway Company. Mr Ferguson said the crossing would be injurious to the port of Port Carlisle.

With none of the directors at the meeting, the letter was simply taken as read.

Joseph didn't give up. He exchanged a series of letters with the Board of Trade in the summer of 1864.

The first asked the BoT to insist, if they had the power, on there being an opening of at least 50-60 feet for vessels to pass through.

He said it was a 'very hard case' on the Port to be so injured, adding that £200,000 had been spent on the docks, harbour, buildings, canal and railway.

He also thought the viaduct could just as easily have been built a quarter of mile east of Port Carlisle.

The Board replied, asking for evidence. They said the average number of vessels 'passaging upwards' did not exceed one in three days, and the largest of them was only 61 tons. The Board also repeated that vessels that size had no problem getting through the Morecambe Bay viaduct. The Board thought a 40 foot gap would be no problem, but anything wider would mean a double span, which would take longer to open and shut and not be as good for passing trade as a single span.

Joseph replied that the average vessels trading to Port Carlisle were 100 tons, and if the tide were running at 7-10 knots per hour, these either would be unable to get through a narrow bridge or would be wrecked against it.

The minimum gap for steam boats and tugs to get through was 60 feet: and if tugs couldn't through to tow vessels, it would be fatal for the Port.

The width of a steam tug (not a large one) presently in Silloth dock was 39 ft 8 inches.

In October 1864, Joseph was informed that the Board had told the Solway Junction Railway Company to provide an opening space 60 feet wide 'in the embankment across the Solway Frith'.

Hope springs

Joseph was delighted, replying that this news had given great satisfaction to residents of Port Carlisle and other interested parties.

In his letters, he had reminded the Board of Trade that large steam boats had for many years been well established at Port Carlisle – and might be again, 'if anything extraordinary happens at Silloth!'

Told you so

Peter's petition got him nowhere, the Bill was passed and the first sod of the new railway was cut on March 28, 1865.

The call to the Lords for the Port Carlisle petitioners to be compensated for injury to their trade or property was rejected. The promise to Joseph wasn't to count for much, either.

Two years later, the House of Commons was told Port Carlisle was barely used as a port now, except by Peter Irving, who lived there and was a ship owner. So, a fixed railway bridge should be substituted for the open bridge proposed in the Bill.

Peter died within months of the viaduct's completion – and if he had managed to keep some vessels still operating from the Port, with him died probably the last person to attempt to do so.

The *Whitehaven News* spelled it out in February 1869, a month after his death: "The viaduct of the Solway Firth had shut up the little place (PC) entirely within itself.

"Sea communication west of the viaduct is quite cut off except for small boats."

A huge feat of engineering

The Solway Viaduct was 1,950 yards long, cost around £100,000, and was completed in 1868. It opened for goods traffic in September 1869, and passengers some time later.

The superstructure consisted of iron lattice girders of 30 ft span, supported on cast-iron columns 12 inches in diameter, sunk in the bed of the Firth to an average depth of 16 ft, the height above the Solway bed averaging 40 ft; the under side of the girders being 8 ft above high water spring tides.

It was then probably the longest viaduct in the UK and contained 1,800 tons of wrought iron and 2,900 tons of cast iron.

Coming from Scotland, trains ran to stations at Bowness, then Whitrigg, Wampool Viaduct, Kirkbride, Abbey Junction, Bromfield, and Brayton Domain Colliery.

Beaten by the weather

The viaduct was damaged by gales and frost on no fewer than 30 occasions. The most dramatic

was during the Great Freeze of 1880/81, when the Eden and Esk froze.

The thaw, at the end of January 1881, saw huge slabs of ice carried down the Solway by the tide, hitting and shaking the pillars of the viaduct, until it started to collapse.

Some 45 of the 193 piers collapsed.

It was rebuilt and back in use by May 1884, but as the iron ore trade declined, its days were numbered.

Failure, and tragedy

The viaduct closed to traffic on August 31, 1921 – it needed more than £70,000 of repairs to make it safe for further use, which simply wasn't viable.

It may not have been connected to the Port, but the story was really the same: high hopes of a great enterprise dashed by income not living up to

This gorse-covered ridge carried the old rail line

expectations, and the company running it getting into debt.

It stood there, perhaps ornamental and certainly an interesting walkway for the brave and adventurous, until May 1934, when demolition began.

This was a far from easy task, and was to cost the lives of three men employed by a Glasgow demolition company. George Walker, 24, of Annan, Walter Morgan of Barrhead, and William Adam, of Carstairs, were drowned after the boat they were working from broke free from the pillar it was tied to, was swept into mid-channel, and overturned. Adam's body was found the next day, and Morgan's soon after.

How it ended

The demolition took 18 months, not helped by the discovery that stones sunk to protect it had created an artificial reef. It was some years before this shipping hazard was completely broken up and dispersed.

The remains of the viaduct can still be seen today. Gorse bushes and other scrub have taken over the railway track bed and embankment leading to them. The marshland is an obstacle course of water courses and holes, and one has to respect the Solway tides. A safe – and dry! – way to get an idea of it is to look at Google's satellite map. The satellite view of the Solway is strange and fascinating. And the two sides of the old line can be seen clearly.

There might be more to see, but for Hitler.

In 1942, the *Newcastle Journal* reported: 'Big scrap find by women'. Women spotters looking for scrap iron for the war effort were well pleased with their visit to Bowness. Among the salvage they chalked up was: railway lines and other parts of the viaduct;

a tractor; two solid metal wheels weighting about 20 hundredweight each, and; the disused railway station at Port Carlisle, 'about which there is a good quantity of scrap iron'.

Those concerned – united by more than business

Peter Irving, being a relative of mine, AND a key figure in Port Carlisle's history, gets his own chapter.

James Hastie

I think James Hastie, the master mariner of 1864, has to be the James who got his master's certificate in 1851. If so, he was born in Ruthwell, Dumfries, in 1797, which fits a man who knew the Solway from the Annan perspective. He looks to have died in Annan in 1874.

Thomas As(h)bridge
Born 1801. died 1887

The ancient mariner, as it were, was born in Maryport. Wife Ann, who died in 1890 'of Drumburgh House,' was the daughter of Richard Lawson, of Drumburgh. They married at Bowness in 1849. In 1871, they were at Drumburgh House, where Thomas is listed as a retired ship owner. He is buried at St Michael's.

One can only wonder what he thought of his pro-viaduct evidence with hindsight.

William Bousfield Page.
Born circa 1818, died 1886

At the 1864 half-yearly meeting of the Port Carlisle Dock and Railway Company, only W B Page and John Nanson showed up. John featured in the canal chapter. He and William B were a little more than business colleagues.

In June 1844, William Bousfield Page (father James) married Ann Ferguson Nanson.

William, born around 1818 in Kent, was a surgeon at Cumberland Infirmary, county jail, and visiting surgeon at the joint counties lunatic asylum, and was also a JP. He added the role of surgeon to the London and North West and other railway companies to that list.

In 1851, he, Ann, three children and four domestics, were living in Devonshire Street, Carlisle. By 1871, they had moved to Lowther Street, and in 1881, they were living in Stainton (Carlisle). When he died in 1886, his personal estate was worth around £92,000.

His wife Ann was born in Carlisle in 1821, the daughter of William and Elizabeth (née Ferguson) Nanson. It's possible that W B Page and John Nanson were brothers-in-law.

Meanwhile...

Joseph Ferguson
Born circa 1795. Died 1880.

Joseph Ferguson wrote the letter, saying the viaduct would harm the Port. He also wrote several letters to the Board of Trade, in the summer of 1864. He was then living in Lowther Street, Carlisle.

Finding out anything about him took a lot of digging, including scrolling through the 1851 the hard way. Not helped by there being another Joseph in town – who was for a while a city MP.

MP Joseph lived in Fisher Street from at least 1827 (next to the Methodist chapel, and next door to John Nanson in 1851). He was in the cotton trade for some years, in a family business, with dye and other works in the city and at Cummersdale.

He died in 1863, so clearly didn't write the 1864 letters, although he was on the canal committee for a while.

'Our' Joseph was an original director of the canal – he was on the original committee in 1819.

He was possibly of English Street in 1825 – unless that was MP Joseph – and was of Abbey Street in 1836.

In 1838, a list of subscriptions to the hand loom weavers includes some familiar names: Peter Dixon, W James MP, W Marshall MP, PH Howard MP, WN Hodgson... but also Joseph Ferguson of Fisher Street and J Ferguson of Abbey Street.

Likewise, in January 1839, there was a dreadful hurricane which caused a swathe of damage from Dublin to York. The damage in Carlisle included a wall collapsing next to Jos Ferguson's house in Fisher Street, and all the rear windows of Joseph Ferguson's house in Abbey Street being forced in. (the chimney at MP Joseph's dye works at Cummersdale was blown down, and the roof of Messrs Ferguson and Chamber's wareroom lost almost all its slates).

By 1841, 'our' Joseph was living in Lowther Street, with his wife Margaret, infant sons Richard and Charles, and five servants. Joseph is listed as a 'cotton spinner m' – which has to mean 'manufacturer,' as someone actually doing the labour wouldn't have had servants.

Two Joseph Fergusons in the cotton trade suggests perhaps he and MP Joseph were cousins?

In 1845, he and William Nanson visited Cumberland Infirmary, and he was re-elected on to the canal company committee. MP Joseph joined the committee a few months later.

43

A Joseph was chairman of Lowther Street Baptist Church in 1848. And a Joseph was chairman of the Mechanics Institute that year – he contributed £100 towards premises for the institute in 1850.

Joseph attended an inquiry into the sanitary conditions in Carlisle in November 1849, and was still in Lowther Street in the summer of 1850.

In 1851, he was at 32 Lowther Street, a 56-year-old widower and a JP. Retired from business, proprietor of houses and land.

With him are sons Richard Saul, 13, and Charles John, 11; visitor Mary Ferguson, single, 61; brother John, 57, merchant (retired from, as above), a cook and two housemaids.

In 1871, he and Charles (now an architect) are at 74 Lowther Street. He died at Lowther Street on June 13, 1880 – late enough to have seen his fears for Port Carlisle realised.

Joseph is listed on the census as having been born in Carlisle. For sure, a Joseph was baptised in Holm Cultram in 1795 (born 1791, place of birth not specified), to William Ferguson and Fanny (née Grave). A Betty was baptised the same day, in 1795).

If Elizabeth Ferguson who married William Nanson was Joseph's sister, then Ann Page was Joseph's niece. And John Nanson likely his nephew.

Meanwhile, son Richard's middle name is a 'giveaway': Joseph's wife Margaret (they married in 1835) was née Margaret Saul. a Margaret was baptised in 1801, daughter of Silas Saul and Jane (Jackson). Which makes her sister of George, of Brunstock House, who didn't want the canal to be filled in.

A history of Port Carlisle shows just how entwined the key figures were, by marriage.

The city end of the canal (then railway), and a reminder that Port Carlisle's creation was due to city manufacturers and politicians

7

A few statistics

THE FOLLOWING are extrapolated
from the census returns – if the
numbers don't add up or make sense,
blame the enumerators!

Bear in mind that prior to the canal
being built there were just the two
dwellings: the Binnacle Inn and Kirkland
House farm – ie, two families, plus their
domestic/farm servants.

These figures don't include Kirkland
House, which from 1851 was
considered part of Drumburgh.

An old postcard showing part of the bowling green, railway
line, and Front Street

Year	Households	Uninhabited	Population
1841	43	-	225
1851	44	4	180
1861	38	12	175
1871	39	20	119
1881	41	1	154
1891	40	11	155
1901	33	20	123
1911	33	-	107

Occupations

Again, the following are taken from the census returns. I've grouped some together (eg all types of labourer, all types of domestic servant). I've also, until 1901, included retired people under their old trade or profession.

1841

• 27 occupations. There are 18 people listed as male/female servant, and 12 labourers/agricultural labourers. There are 12 mariners*, three customs officers/excise officers/tide waiters and a harbourmaster, two lock-keepers, and a warehouseman. There are also three shoemakers and three apprentices.

1851

• 29 occupations. Main one: mariner: 16. Domestic servants: 8. Labourers: 7. There's a ship owner (Peter Irving), a shipwright, a deputy harbour master, a customs officer, and two tide waiters**. The three joiners and the cooper may have been connected to the port.

1861

• 21 occupations. There are 12 labourers (highest), and 11 mariners. There are still a shipwright, a ship's carpenter, a harbourmaster, and Peter Irving the ship owner. Others are a broad mix, including what appears to be a 'kipperman' (hard to read), and the oddest being, clearly written, 'retired lodger' (Elizabeth Mackereth, *see chapter on the seaside*)!

1871

• 21 occupations. Main ones: mariner: 8. Yeoman/farmer/retired farmer: 5. There's a

customs officer, and a railway station agent, plus a porter.

1881

• 21 occupations. Main ones: fisherman: 10. Domestics (housekeepers, servants etc): 8. There are three 'taylors' with two apprentices. There are four mariners. And a station master and two railway servants.

1891

• 19 occupations. And it's a tie for the top between fishermen and people living on independent means (annuitants, etc): 10 each. There's also one greyhound trainer, one station agent – and a Dandy driver – as there will be in 1901 and 1911.

1901

• 25 occupations. There are ten people who are retired, three clerks, a solicitor, and an architect. Enumerator Edward Lawson Irving (Peter's son) is an assistant — with the word 'local' scribbled over the rest. There are still four fishermen, and two water bailiffs, but the only mariners are retired.

1911

• 24 occupations. And with nine (of the 33) households headed by a woman, the single biggest occupation, at six, is dressmaker. There are five haaf net fishermen, and two water bailiffs, but no mariners. There's also (*see chapter on the seaside*), a man called Henry Harrop, who at 36 has filled in his occupation as 'retired pensioner'.

* I have counted 'mariner's wife' as effectively 'mariner' where the husband is absent (away at sea).

** A tide waiter was an inspector who boarded ships on arrival to enforce customs regulations

8

Oh, I do like to be beside the seaside

In its heyday, Port Carlisle was a popular holiday resort

AT THE start of the chapter on Silloth, I used two small photos of family members enjoying themselves there in the 1930s.

There are other photos in the album that include a car, so it looks like they had driven there, from their farm in the Eden Valley – bypassing Port Carlisle.

The branch line to Port Carlisle had shut on May 31 (or June 1) 1932 – despite some protest.

There had been protest meetings, a deputation, an appeal to the minister of transport, and local MPs had tried to do something – but all in vain. The closure was blamed on competition by motor buses making the line unprofitable – something that was to lead to the closure of a lot more rail lines, a trend most famously associated with the infamous Beeching Cuts of the 1960s.

You could still rent a bedroom and sitting room (with attendance) to stay there. But I suspect Silloth had more to offer in the way of family amusement. The bowling club were active, as were the haaf-net fishermen. And you could go bird-watching, or

marvel at how fast the tide came in. But Port Carlisle's heyday as a seaside resort was long past.

The treacherous Solway

It's not like it had ever been a safe place to take the children. I've mentioned, in the chapter on Peter Irving, one tragedy when children wading out into the Solway were caught out by a trench. And the tide doesn't just come in fast, it can come in behind the unwary day-tripper.

Two Wigan boys – William Beattie and John Wilkinson – were lucky in 1852. Told it was safe to wade over to Port Carlisle, they soon found it wasn't.

Luckily, they were able to swim, their cries were heard, and a boat rescued them.

An example with a fortunate ending occurred in July 1937, when two Carlisle 15-year-olds were marooned on a sandbank, terrified as the waters rose. Margaret Stewart and Vera Dunkeld, who had been paddling at Port Carlisle but gone out too far, said they prayed in the face of certain death. Their prayers were answered. A motorist on the Scottish shore, scanning the firth through binoculars, saw their plight. He drove for help and fisherman Duncan and John Bryson rowed out to rescue the girls rescued, the water by now up to their chins.

Another account of the drama says the motorist saw them through a telescope, but that it was two holidaymakers camping at Eastriggs who gave the alarm. It says Vera was 16, and the girls had lost their sense of direction, effectively trying to walk right across the firth instead of turning back to Port Carlisle. The holidaymakers said they'd heard a large crowd shouting on the shore, and seen the girls waving and shouting in the middle of the firth.

The fishermen rowed the girls back to the English shore, where they received attention at a farmhouse, before being taken home.

Whatever the full truth of the story, the Solway has always been somewhere to treat with great respect – and no place at all for non-swimmers.

Baths in a superior style

The baths at Port Carlisle never came close to matching those at Allonby. The latter were opened in 1835 (in that 'fashionable watering place') and are described as comprising warm, cold, shower and vapour baths, library, and an elegant assembly room opening upon a balcony promenade… The baths are of marble, fitted up on the newest principle, and the the supply of water, properly filtered, is brought from the sea every tide by means of steam power.'

Allonby was also possibly a 'safer' place to take impressionable young people! At least according to a story in 1842 that there was a ferryman named Joseph Brough 'opposite Bowness' who was said to be carrying out eight or nine irregular marriages a week. He'd row over to Port Carlisle from the Scottish side, pick the couple up, and act as priest (it wasn't just Gretna hosted such marriages, by any means).

It was in 1843 that a joint-stock company was formed to establish public baths at Port Carlisle. The aim was to raise £500, in £5 shares, and upwards of seventy were quickly taken. The intended site was close to the hotels and jetty and would be filled by filtering seawater. There were to be three baths for hot or cold bathing, and three shower baths.

It was hoped to open them by September – with a new terrace nearby.

Hope springing eternal in Port Carlisle, it was felt there was every reason to expect it would become the most-popular of all the bathing resorts on the coast.

An update in mid-September said they should be open in a matter of days, but no one seems to have reported on the actual opening.

However, in April 1844, William Wood was advertising that he had taken on the management of the baths, which he declared 'have been fitted up by the committee of management in a style superior to any similar establishment in the North.'

I suspect there was a bit of exaggeration about that claim!

A hope realised

The baths were said to be a great accommodation to the public and a source of general attraction to the port. And with the usual hope surrounding all developments at Port Carlisle, it was felt there would be many more visitors that summer, drawn by the attraction of hot and cold salt water bathing.

That summer, the port itself was struggling with a sand problem, rendering the steamer berths, wharfs and warehouses useless. However, as a visitor resort, Port Carlisle was thriving to the point of being crowded.

The Patriot put that down largely to the new baths: 'The arrangements are excellent: the water is beautifully clear, being well filtered before it is used, and yet it retains all the valuable characteristics of sea water.

'The parties in attendance are remarkably civil and attentive and the inducement thus given to the public is so strong that lodgings are now very difficult to meet with and in fact, a number of new houses are immediately required.'

Port Carlisle, in the summer of 1845, was a thriving watering place, crowded with visitors from the city.

And the following year, the Carlisle and Liverpool Steam Navigation Company commissioned the building of a first-class iron steamer to run between Port Carlisle, Annan, and Liverpool, in eight hours, to meet the growing wants of Port Carlisle and district.

Shares worth having

Carlisle at that time had a House of Recovery: a fever hospital. It took patients with illnesses such as typhoid, scarlet fever, smallpox, etc. It was a charitable institution, with an annual meeting of subscribers. At the December 1846 AGM, a letter was read out from Carlisle MP Philip Howard, apologising for his absence (he was in London). After praising the valuable work of the House of Recovery, he said he would be making over his shares in the Port Carlisle Baths, upon which a dividend would shortly be payable.

He had four £5 shares, which were welcomed by the committee as a handsome donation.

The House of Recovery's annual accounts the following year show the dividend it received on those shares was 16 shillings.

An advert in May 1848 offered an unspecified number of shares for sale, with no clue as to the price. What it DID provide was the name: the Victoria Baths, Port Carlisle.

That summer was another good one. By June, visitors were arriving in increasing numbers. A new boiler had been installed, the water was always clear, and under the attentive superintendence of Mrs Murray, a delightful hot dip might be obtained at a few minutes' notice.

And that year, the House of Recovery's shares earned it £1 in dividends.

In August 1849, Allonby was 'gay,' Flimby was 'full,' and Port Carlisle and Bowness were exhibiting 'more than wonted bustle' (according to the Patriot).

The House of Recovery didn't mention its shares, but a meeting of the proprietors of the baths was held in Carlisle the following February, at which a dividend of three per cent was declared, payable by Edward Jobling, the treasurer.

The city mayor, Joseph Rome, along with R Cowen, WR Martindale, Joseph Hope, and C Thurnham were appointed as the management committee for the coming year.

Also in February 1850, the Hope and Anchor (plus its yard, garden, stabling, piggery, and every necessary appurtenance) were put up for auction (now in the occupation of Mrs E Carlton). 'Also will be sold, same time, one share in the Victoria Baths, at Port Carlisle'.

Under new management

So far, the names of William Wood, then Mrs Murray had appeared as actually running the baths (as it were). In March 1850, they were advertised as being to let for 12 months from April (apply to Edward Jobling, Navigation Office, Carlisle).

Whoever took it over had a less successful season than his or her predecessors, as the House of Recovery's dividends that December were just 12 shillings.

It was perhaps because of this that the following season, there was an announcement of the Great Reduction in Prices. Along with the assurance that the baths had just been put in good order. Apply Mrs Murray, Canal Cottage, adjoining baths.

The rates were:

- Hot baths. Single bath 1s 6d; four baths 5s; Upwards 1s 3d each.

- Cold baths. Single bath 9d; five baths 2s 6d; Upwards 6d each.

- Shower baths. Each bath 6d.

I have no idea what 'upwards baths' were! The House of Recovery accounts sadly aren't any help that year or thereafter (as far as I checked).

All quiet, but pass the lemonade

There don't seem to be any mentions of the baths over the next few years. On August 1, 1853, the canal closed, and work started on draining it, for work to start on the railway.

That put paid to those who had taken advantage of the pleasure trips along the canal to visit Port Carlisle from the city. It also put paid to steamers putting in at Port Carlisle (if the sand situation would let them anyway).

It was to be June 1854 before the railway opened for passengers and steamers could think of returning. Did that have much effect on custom?

The railway brought with it hopes of Port Carlisle thriving as a holiday resort, to the extend that in May 1854, a Temperance Hotel and Boarding House were opened there, offering 'the most reasonable scale of charges,' along with good bedrooms and well-aired beds.

Dinners and tea and coffee were available on short notice, along with soda water, lemonade, cigars, etc.

Meanwhile, Mrs Wood, proprietress, was also promising well-aired beds at the Solway Hotel, which had 'undergone a thorough repair and now combines every comfort'. Her advert mentions the baths as being 'contiguous to the hotel'. It also says wines and spirits of superior quality are served.

However, that summer also saw the start of something ominous: the railway brought large numbers of day-trippers to Port Carlisle... where they boarded a steamer that took them to Silloth, to see the site of the proposed new docks.

The party arrived back at the Port just after 8pm, and returned to Carlisle at 9pm. They may have had something to eat and drink at the Port's inns/hotels, but it probably wasn't much after the 'ample cold collation' they'd had at lunchtime. And there was no need for the beds to be aired, or the baths to be ready to run, at all.

Another attraction

While aimed at benefiting residents more than visitors, this section is probably the best place to mention Port Carlisle's reading room and library.

The facility was set up in January 1855, the use of a room having been granted to its members by the directors of Port Carlisle Dock and Railway.

Early donations included: 10s from Robert Elliot MD; the Leisure Hour (weekly) and five volumes from I F Whitridge; four volumes from James Barnes, and two volumes from R Robinson.

Miss E Wood gave £1, as did Peter Irving. J Irving gave six volumes; J Bell two, and: T Peat seven.

A month later, the members were grateful for donations: R Ferguson (mayor) £1; Rev J Norman 10s; W Borrowdale 10s; Mrs Waite 5s; A Well-wisher seven volumes; Mrs Hudson three volumes; J Irving one volume; D Moore one volume. William Marshall MP later gave £1.

William James of Barrock Park (familiar to the Port for chairing the canal and railway company committees) presented the reading room with 19 volumes (on history and biography, among other topics)

In 1856, he presented the reading the room with a copy of The British Workman for 1855. This wasn't a book but an 'improving' magazine launched in 1855 by Methodist reformer and Temperance campaigner Thomas Bywater Smithies. It contained wood-cut illustrations, moralising poems, and articles on leading a good and useful life.

There were other kinds of donation as well: in November 1855, Mrs Thompson of Kirkhouse contributed half a waggon of coals.

Hotels to let – and an Oriental Temple

There are few references to the Temperance Hotel, beyond a one-line 'to sell or let' advert in July 1856 (when the hotel should surely have been busy): apply T Mackereth, grocer, Carlisle. He inserted a 'for sale' advert three years later for a house at Port Carlisle: 'suitable for an inn'. I suspect it was the same property.

In May 1855, Mrs Wood advertised the Solway Hotel as being to let, for such a term of years as may be agreed on. It was the first of what were to be a series of such adverts, which suggest it wasn't proving a profitable enough enterprise to keep its owner, or subsequent tenants, happy.

James Boyle was first to take it on, late in 1855. His advert announcing the fact mentions its proximity to the baths – and to the Oriental Temple. Which I've not found references to anywhere else.

But during his first summer, as the Silloth railway neared completion, its backers were proclaiming they would be opening up a bathing place for the inhabitants of Carlisle that would present more advantages, on better terms, than any other bathing place which they at present enjoyed.

And in January 1857, the Solway Hotel was to let: apply Mrs Wood or the tenant. This was followed by various offers to sell or let the place. These included suggestions such as letting it for the summer months upon terms of a private house, or as a lodging house, or as private apartments.

As well as commanding an extensive view of the Scotch (sic) hills, it says *Port Carlisle is a summer resort not to be equalled in Cumberland. The jetty 'is in front of the door, extending 300-400 yards into the Solway.*

'The purity of the air is too well-known to require comment.

'Hot and cold baths to hand.'

A going-nowhere concern

It doesn't seem like there were any takers, for it was still being advertised for sale or to let – and was still in the occupation of Mr Boyle – right through 1858 and into 1859.

Mr Boyle finally gave up, with a huge auction of July 27 of all the furniture, bar fittings, crockery and so on. A sale that was right at what should have been the height of the season.

By then, Silloth had a new hotel, was gaining a reputation for its salubrious climate and pure air, and had set a site aside to build a sea-bathing establishment (work to build it had for sure started by September, and it was completed by the start of the 1860 season).

In 1860, there is an advert for 'most spacious and comfortable apartments' at Solway View House. It says Port Carlisle is well-known for the purity of the air, 'and is free from the indiscriminate confusion of cheap trips, and over-crowding.'

This was probably just a dig a Silloth: cheap trips in summer were a twice-weekly offer in adverts by the Silloth railway company. But it does rather suggest Port Carlisle was losing out heavily on the tourist trade.

The Binnacle, by the way, looks to have ceased being a pub some time before 1851.

The Ship Inn, Port Carlisle, was advertised to let in 1860, due to death of the landlady, but probably stayed a pub for a while, at least.

'Still in perfect order'

Port Carlisle Baths were still going in the summer of 1863, 'in perfect order and easily accessible'.

Plunge baths were 9d; shower baths 6d; hot baths 1s 6d; with a 3d discount for three baths or more. Peter Irving's son James was the honorary secretary of the company, in Carlisle. The advert appeared in the *Carlisle Journal* in May and through June. The wording 'offer an excellent opportunity to any one requiring them' isn't a great advertising slogan, implying the baths were of limited interest rather than appealing to all.

By 1867, Peter had become the honorary secretary, but the advert is otherwise unchanged.

Useful information for burglars

By 1884, Cumbrian newspapers had taken to publishing lists of holidaymakers – complete with their home addresses. A listing in June that year says a Mrs Milburn, of Portland Place, Carlisle, was staying at Miss Rome's. Meanwhile, Mrs Toppin (Solway View) was hosting Mrs Hudson and family, and Mrs Irving, from Bootle, Liverpool, and: Mrs M McLean and family, Brae House, Annan.

And that was it for Port Carlisle.

There are dozens of entries for Silloth.

A similar list in August 1891 has something like 18 families or individuals staying at Port Carlisle. The entries for Silloth take up almost a full column in the (broadsheet) *Carlisle Express and Examiner*. And other such listings paint a similar picture.

When did it end?

Things go quiet in relation to the baths after 1867. A photo of Mary J Irving in the boiler room is a puzzle. The only Mary J on the census is the wife of Edward Lawson Irving.

But at some point in the 1890s, the building was converted into a house. For on the 1911 census, there is one Henry Harrop, 36, (born Hanley, Staffs), with a wife and two not-obviously-related-to-them teenager visitors.

Henry's occupation is the puzzling (given his age) 'retired pensioner'.

He gives his address as Bath House, Port Carlisle.

The bath house has remained a private residence to this day, having been owned by the same family since 1944.

As for the resort...

When the Dandy made its last trip in April 1914, it was hoped this would 'open up' the district as a resort.

The *Carlisle Journal* said: "The inhabitants expect that the two villages will in future enjoy still greater prosperity as holiday resorts under the improved conditions of travelling."

However, the local papers warned it would take more than a steam train to attract day-trippers and holidaymakers: it needed 'means of recreation'.

The bowling green was one attraction, but while the village was attractive, and offered country walks as well as the seashore, it had a difficult task competing with other coastal resorts.

And there were other important schemes needed to be carried out if the village was ever going to attract large numbers in summer – starting with a good water supply.

Carlisle was willing to supply water on reasonable terms, and people interested in the village's welfare would 'do well to raise their voices against unreasonable delay'.

A further deterrent was that by then, there was almost nowhere left for visitors to stay.

No one would build amenities (a golf course was mooted) if there was little accommodation for holidaymakers. And no one would build hotels without amenities to attract visitors.

Who's who

William Wood and Mrs Wood

An 1829 directory lists a William Wood at Kirkland House, and on the 1841 census, there was a William Wood there, born about 1796, yeoman. He had a wife Mary, ten years younger, and with them were Mary 15, Jane 13, Elizabeth 11, Alice 9, and Martha 6.

William and Mary were still there ten years later, although the age difference between them has been cut to six years (probably from the 1841 practice of rounding adult ages up or down to the nearest five years). William, born in Yorkshire, is farming 190 acres. He had died by December 1854, when Sarah, his eldest daughter, married Captain James Hudson.

Was it this William who took over managing the baths in 1844?

As for 'Mrs Wood'… she was the owner of Old Binnacle in 1855 (when she was described as 'of the Lowther Arms Hotel, at Port Carlisle'), and; in 1857, when she sought to sell or let the Solway Hotel. In June 1859, she advertised the Binnacle to let: a dwelling with garden, stable and out offices, in her occupation. Ditto March 1860.

Sadly, the census returns are no help proving if Mrs Wood was Mary. The Binnacle had been let by 1861, to a young couple called Hutchinson. There is a widowed Mary, 60, 'property of house and land,' living in Port Carlisle, but no house name

By 1868, Mrs Wood was living at Solway View: that May, she sold up the contents, prior to leaving the neighbourhood. The contents were those of a private house, but included a bathing box – and an iron pump with about 25 feet of lead piping.

Mrs Murray

We know a Mrs Murray was supervising the baths in 1848, and living at Canal Cottage. The only candidate on the 1851 census is a Frances, aged 42, born Scotland. The address isn't detailed beyond Port Carlisle. Her husband, William Murray, 44, was the deputy harbour master. 1841 doesn't give a detailed address either, but tells us William was then a lock keeper – which would seem to fit someone living at a place called Canal Cottage. They were still at Port Carlisle in 1861 (see also the fishing chapter).

Elizabeth Carl(e)ton

Mrs E Carlton was at the Hope and Anchor in 1850, and is listed on the census in 1851 as a 'licenced vitealor' (sic). Widowed, aged 34, her (also widowed) mother Elizabeth Withering-- was living with her.

In January 1846, she threw a man called Thompson out of the pub, refusing to serve him with drink. His wife Elizabeth Thompson broke a window at the pub (and was ordered to pay 1s 6d, plus costs). Mrs Thompson admitted the damage, but pleaded great provocation from 'the encouragement her husband received' at the pub.

Elizabeth C held an annual ball in Port Carlisle, including one on December 31, 1856 (tea on the table at 6pm).

A William Carlton, innkeeper, drowned in the Solway in 1843 – but his wife on the 1841 census was Isabella.

Elizabeth Carlton remarried, in October 1857, Glasson yeoman John Sharp. They lived at Port Carlisle after, John being listed as an innkeeper in 1861 and a grocer ten years later. John Sharp is the right age to have been the son of Jeremiah Sharp (see the chapters on fishing, and Westfield House).

James Boyle

James Boyle was doing his best to make a go of the Solway Hotel from 1855-59. It seems unlikely he was a local, as there is no sign of him on the census returns.

The 1850 management committee

These all seem to have been Carlisle men – they were headed by the city mayor, Joseph Rome.

R Cowen is a puzzle. William R Martindale was a 61-year-old druggist, in English Street, Carlisle. Joseph Hope was probably a Carlisle wine merchant. C Thurnham seems likely to have been Charles, the printer.

Thomas Mackereth

Born circa 1820, died 1902

The Carlisle grocer behind the Temperance Hotel advert in 1856. In 1862, there is a 'for sale by auction' advert for 13-room dwelling house at Port Carlisle, 'at present occupied by Thomas Mackereth'. He was living in Carlisle on the 1851-91 censuses inclusive, so presumably it was his mother Elizabeth (below)'s house; unless it was the hotel and he'd failed to sell in 1859.

Thomas Mackereth, of 52 English Street, Carlisle, offered (in 1855) lemons, oranges, raisins, figs, dates, walnuts… 'pineapples and grapes can be had by giving a few days' notice'. He also stocked Polson's Imperial Patent Starch, and Du Barry's Delicious Health Restoring Revalenta Arabic Food (cures dyspepsia, indigestion, lung disease, partial deafness, nervousness, low spirits and nervous fancies).

He was also a shipping agent for clippers on the Australia run (and elsewhere).

And by 1901, he was living in Kendal – as the proprietor of a Temperance Hotel.

Thomas was born around 1820 at Bank Ground, Coniston, to a John and Elizabeth.

Elizabeth Mackereth

Born circa 1786, died 1861

Under one of Thomas' adverts, an E Mackereth, meanwhile, assured that visitors to Port Carlisle

could be supplied with bread, biscuits, buns, tea cakes, and all kinds of confectionery, lemonade, etc.

Widowed Elizabeth Mackereth died in June 1861, at Port Carlisle, aged 75. Born in Bowness, an 1847 directory lists her as a grocer in Port Carlisle. She appears as the same on the 1841 census, with Jane, 25, Ann, 22, and Esther, 19, and Ann 86, listed after her.

Ann Mackereth senior died in 1843, her age then recorded as 92 – her grave (very hard to read) at St Michael's names her as widow of the late Thomas, of Bank Ground, Coniston.

When daughter Jane (by then Mrs Reade) visited her in 1851, Jane's place of birth was listed as North Plain.

Elizabeth Mackereth's 1861 will (widow of Port Carlisle) names daughters Elizabeth Druikall, Jane Reed (sic), Ann Richardson, and Esther. They get £50 each and things like pillows and beds.

Son Thomas is the main beneficiary, getting the real estate, and the family silver (two silver salts, six teaspoons, and the tea tongs).

Philip Howard MP

Born 1801, died 1883

Philip Howard features in this chapter because he bought, and later donated to charity, four shares in the baths. He was related to the dukes of Norfolk and his family home was Corby Castle. He was (a

Whig) MP for Carlisle from 1830-1847, and 1848-1852.

A lot of the political supporters of the canal, the railway, the Solway ports, and in this case the baths, were Whigs. It certainly explains why the initially pro-canal Carlisle Patriot became a strong critic of Solway projects (the canal committee's run-in with Lord Lonsdale over the troublesome jetty can't have endeared it to the Patriot, either).

Joseph Brough

Died 1851

Joseph Brough was the priest-ferryman, who lived on the Scottish side of the Solway, but is getting a mention here because of the tragic end to his career.

In August 1851, he made the crossing from Port Carlisle with five passengers. They were Walter Park, an Annan draper; his late partner, John Scott; Mrs Scott; Anthony Nelson, a Port Carlisle draper, and; John Beck, a farm servant.

Despite having made the crossing thousands of times, over the course of 50 years, on this occasion Joseph Brough was too late starting and the boat tangled with nets set between Whinnyrigg and Seafield.

The boat overturned.

Walter Park and Anthony Nelson managed somehow to cling to the nets, and were rescued. The other four drowned. Mr Scott's body wasn't recovered.

A sad scene

As a postscript to this chapter, I think it's well worth summarising an opinion piece that appeared in the *Carlisle Journal* in August 1865.

I've left it for the end as it seems to sum up the chapter.

"It is curious to notice the rise and fall of certain places of resort at the seaside in the popular estimation. One year it is Bowness and the Port; next year Allonby and Skinburness are the most attractive; and then Silloth comes forward and sweeps all the health seekers into its capacious maw."

Apart from building sandcastles, bathing (ladies could 'bob up and down with the comfort of Jonathan Nichol's bathing boxes'), and eating toffee, a big attraction at Allonby was apparently watching the tide come in. Which fair enough, is something of a spectacle for anyone not used to it, although the writer was

Tempting to walk on, anything but safe

somewhat sarcastic about it.

The writer then looks back to the time, 'not long ago,' when Bowness and the Port rivalled Allonby as seaside resorts.

He describes the lively scene of the Port Carlisle's docks, with ships of assorted sizes busying about their business. You could watch American timber vessels unload at the stone pier, or the funnels of steamers belching smoke, while passengers disembarked and merchandise was unloaded. Meanwhile, the Arrow (boat) would bring passengers down the canal from Carlisle.

The author says most of the houses in Front Street were filled with visitors.

But by the summer of 1865, all had changed.

"The canal is filled up; the Arrow is laid by; the steam-boats have ceased to ply; the harbour is silted up; the trade of the Port has departed, and;

the shipping list records only the movement of the Black Diamond, Hastie, Annan.

"Even the pavilion which for some years yawned in vain for visitors who never came has now gone to seek a more popular habitation.

"The Port, its docks and jetties, present a sad scene of desolation. The (Solway) hotel is converted into a private house; a few invalids are generally all the visitors who are to be seen about the place; the arrivals and departures of the Dandy – sometimes without a single passenger – are the great events of each day and call forth the population to the front doors; while the coming of the rural postman is a downright excitement."

On the up side, the author writes (of Bowness) of being able to enjoy the pleasure of the country with the benefits of the seaside, and that it's a great place to appreciate birdlife, and to seek repose and solitude. A fact which led to the RSPB setting up a reserve at Campfield Marsh (North Plain) in 1987.

9

Not so fine and Dandy

NO HISTORY of Port Carlisle could be complete without mentioning that curious invention the Dandy. For one thing, it was from the start, truly a curiosity. For another, it symbolises again how high hopes of transforming Port Carlisle (by the canal, by the railway) were doomed almost before the celebration cake had been finished.

The short version is that the regular passenger rail service from the Drumburgh-to-Port-Carlisle branch line (as it became from August 1856) proved uneconomic. So, it was replaced with the quaint and slightly bonkers idea of a carriage pulled on the rail tracks by a horse.

Finding accurate information on the history of the Dandy cars has proved tricky: different sources suggest different dates for its introduction, and disagree on how many Dandy cars there were over the years (three/four?) and when they were introduced.

Not wishing to print misinformation, I'll leave it for others to come up with a definitive history. This book is, after all, focussing more on people and the spirit of the place than technical details about masts on sailing ships, or classes of steam engine.

Hello Dandy, but when?

When did the Dandy make its first run? One source says 1856 (as soon as the Silloth line opened),

The Dandy was a popular subject on postcards

another 1857, a third 1861, a fourth 1863. Perhaps it depends on when the name 'Dandy' was first applied. Some sources say Dandy no 1 was built in 1859 (replacing the first horse-drawn carriage on the line), others say 1863 (others again say 1863 was

Dandy no 2, which seems to have been replaced in 1908).

In October 1856, the railway company had sought tenders for an engine shed, tank house and carriage shed. And not long after, a 16-year-old stoker called Edward Cartner was fatally injured when he fell reboarding his engine and was run over by a waggon. (There are two candidates on the 1851 census). But was this on the PC branch, or the main line?

In March 1857, William James announced that thanks to the Silloth line opening, the Port Carlisle Railway had taken about £1,000 extra in the first half of its financial year.

This was confirmed at the AGM in July, when it was shown the receipts for the year had been £5,139 (it had been £3,699 the previous year, and £2,220 in its first year).

"Should the revenue of the company continue to increase in the above ration, there can be no doubt that the line, though at present unremunerative from the large amount of interest now payable, will ere long become a remunerative undertaking."

It says the company supplies the engine power for the Silloth line as well, and has three engines: one tank engine, and two new, powerful tender engines.

The report has a go at the Patriot's doom-mongering, and says there were 53,135 passengers over the last year (up from 37,800 the year before). Of course, from August 1856, the first eight-and-a-half miles of the PC railway had been used by trains going to Silloth.

There is no breakdown of how many of the 53,135 passengers were going to Silloth and how many to Port Carlisle.

The 1858 AGM said receipts had risen to £6,178.

Mr James said the time was now approaching when any troubles and difficulties against which they had to content would be terminated, and that at no very distant period they would arrive at that goal of prosperity which they had so long been struggling and striving to reach.

One can only hope the Patriot's error in reporting that bit of the speech truly was accidental: the paper printed 'arrive at that gaol' rather than 'goal'!

In fact, so optimistic (carried away) was he, that Mr James spoke of 'ere long' being able to pay not only the interest on the loans etc taken out to build the railway, but also to pay the bondholders interest. He went so far as to hold out hope for the original canal shareholders (now railway shareholders). Though he did warn them they'd have to wait for the Silloth Dock to open, and the new rail line from Port Carlisle to Hawick to see their canal shares restored 'to something like their former value'.

As for the Port – the state of the channel at Port Carlisle was now 'better than it had ever been within the memory of man', and the state of trade at the port was better than it had been for a long time.

Whether the improvement in the channel was down to the removal of Lord Lonsdale's jetty, or their own efforts in removing obstructions, he would not say.

Horse-drawn for sure

I found a trespass case in October 1858 that refers to 'the carriage which takes passengers between Drumburgh and Port Carlisle'.

One version says Isaac Brown, seed merchant of Carlisle, was charged with trespass on the line on August 18. Brown had come to Drumburgh, 'but finding that the carriage, which is drawn by a horse to Port Carlisle, was not there, he walked down the line to the Port'. (He was fined 5s, plus 6s costs). Brown had done the same thing about 12 months earlier – does that suggest the Dandy, or its forerunner, was in operation then? Or was Brown just confident no steam train would run him down as he walked on the track?

Receipts of the PC Railway

The official returns to Parliament in 1859 showed many railways worked at a loss, and all worked at a costly rate in relation to earnings. The report covered traffic earned, working costs, and preference charges for 1858. Of those that submitted returns, 14 showed deficiencies on the year's business done against the year's working and preference charges.

Among these was the Port Carlisle Railway, whose deficiency was set at £1,800. This needs to be borne in mind when reading the revenue figures.

Gross revenue, rounded to nearest pound

•1855: £2,791

•1856: £3,700

•1857: £5,140

•1858: £6,179

•1859: £6,613

•1860: £6,054

•1861: £6,156.

The passenger numbers by 1861 had risen to 76,139, but there's still no breakdown for how many of those actually went to/left from Port Carlisle,

rather than being Silloth passengers using the Carlisle-Drumburgh stretch.

Meanwhile, the net revenue had not once been enough to meet the interest payments due on the company's various forms of borrowings.

The railway company sought to raise money by selling off land that had been purchased to build the canal and/or railway. One 1861 letter offers to sell to Lord Lonsdale land near Drumburgh that the company had bought off Richard Lawson for £46. It's two roods, 12 perches, and the sea side of the railway.

There are other 1861 'offer to sell you land' letters: "directors are anxious to dispose of all surplus lands."

If the original owners didn't want to buy it back, the rail company then offered it to adjoining owners.

Looking at the maps, I think the owners had profited far more from selling it than they would have by keeping it. And can't see why they'd want it back!

At least the running costs were low. A report to the Board of Trade in 1858 put the average working cost of railways per mile, in England and Wales, at £1,564, with 15 per cent going on maintenance.

The Port Carlisle's maintenance costs were £43 per mile. At the upper end of the scale, the North London Railway's maintenance costs were £791 per mile. Of course, feeding a horse was cheaper than stoking a boiler!

There's good news and bad...

At the 1861 AGM, the good news was that the harbour had 'never been in a more favourable state'.

The bad was the financial position of the company was 'less favourable than last year.'

The company had written off (bar £500) some £3,319 in port dues owed by the Silloth Steam Navigation Company Limited. And had to expend £6,000 on erecting a goods shed, offices and coal and lime vaults at Carlisle Station, in anticipation of increased traffic coming from opening of the Border Union Line. The North British Railway's Hawick and Carlisle Extension, about to open, would terminate at (and form a junction with) the Port Carlisle Railway, would use the company's Carlisle station, and its traffic (whether going to Silloth or Carlisle) would pass over sections of the PC railway.

There could be no upbeat speech that year by William James of Barrock Park – instead, there was a brief tribute paid to him and to deputy chairman George Dixon, both having been 'removed by death'.

William's place in the chair was taken by William Marshall MP, who hoped they might have a much more favourable report next year. He regretted William James had not lived long enough to see the railway recover.

A Lieutenant Colonel Maclean said he'd become a shareholder so he could have a say at the meeting, having a heavy stake as a bondholder. He had given up all hope of seeing again anything he had, but now saw the determination of the directors and thought he might get a small return.

Joseph Ferguson (*see the railway chapter*), a shareholder of the both the railway and the canal company, said he was only person living who had been a director of the latter.

He hoped to live to see better days.

Joe, and William James, could have lived a lot longer and not seen better days.

In November 1861, there was a meeting at Carlisle Town Hall to discuss a plan to lease the Port Carlisle Railway to the North British Railway.

PCR preference stocks would become NBR ones; PCR mortgage debts would be converted into debenture stock (and arrears on interest written off); PCR original share capital would receive a guaranteed one per cent dividend in perpetuity; the NBR would pay PCR a rent of £3,100 a year to cover the above interest and dividend and expenses... and so it goes on.

It was the only hope for a company drowning as its net revenue continue to fall well below what it needed to pay the interest on its borrowings. Unsurprisingly, at the extraordinary general meeting, those present voted to grab the opportunity as the best (and only one) they could hope for.

The Bill went through the Houses of Commons and Lords – and through the 'Scotch proceedings in Parliament' – early in 1862 and passed with very little alteration.

The PCR was to lease all its property and undertakings to the NBR for a term of 999 years.

The term, while traditional for leases, was somewhat over-optimistic!

It did mean, however, that in 1864, 1865, 1868, 1869 and 1877 (that I found), the PCR was able to announce dividends for shareholders and debenture holders.

It was mooted, in 1872, that the PCR (and Silloth) railways should amalgamate with the NBR, but it was quickly dropped.

In September 1880, however, both the PCR and the Carlisle & Silloth Railway (along with the North British, Arbroath, and Montrose Railway company) were amalgamated with the NBR.

So, back to the Dandy, then

In case anyone was wondering (I was!) the sleepers of the rail track were covered with a thick layer of ballast, to make life easier for the horses.

Another old postcard marked the first day of the new service, with a 'gaily decked' train

The carriages used over the 50-odd years differed in style and appearance. For example, the 'new Dandy' had three compartments inside – one first class, and two thirds – with luggage put on the roof. On the old Dandy no. 1, it was too low for anyone to stand up inside, but the (up to 12) passengers did at least have shelter from the elements. The (up to 18) third-class passengers sat on the outside.

If someone ran one now, as a heritage attraction, it would no doubt prove very popular. But at the time, I suspect few people appreciated the novelty – especially on a wet winter's day.

Farewell Dandy, on a cloud of fresh optimism

For sure, the last Dandy run was on Saturday, April 4, 1914. And on Monday April 6, it was replaced by a steam train – with all the usual hope and optimism that this would bring people flocking to Port Carlisle – as a holiday resort.

A 'gaily decked' train brought officials of the North British Railway, and guests, to Port Carlisle, and a celebration dinner was laid on for them by Bowness Parish Council.

A postcard sold to mark the launch proclaims that the train carried the Dandy horses as passengers.

Parish council chairman Rev Mitten said while the Dandy would be missed, from a sentimental point of view, everyone welcomed the convenience and comfort the modern means of travel would bring.

Rev Mitten thought the new steam train service would open up the district.

Mr Topping spoke of how steamers used to run between Port Carlisle and Liverpool, and vessels from Quebec and elsewhere sailed up with timber etc.

But the railway over the Solway had effectively stopped all shipping at Port Carlisle, the place sank into decay, and was kept from thriving by the primitive means of travelling.

It would seem Mr T (could this be Christopher, of Westfield House, I wonder?) was rather overlooking the fact the Dandy was only introduced due to low demand for the original rail service!

Mr Black, for the NBR, said the present Dandy had done 51 years of service and its design was a triumph of quaintness.

Mr Reed announced, to applause, that (one) Dandy had been presented to the bowling green.

A day for rejoicing

The local papers claimed there was 'little regret' at the Dandy retiring, saying the Port and Bowness had been 'sadly handicapped in their material development by their primitive means of communication with the outer world'.

The *Carlisle Journal* welcomed the fact that passengers would henceforth travel in a more modern and expeditious fashion: "The Dandy has been severely taxed to cope with the traffic and the inconvenience and slowness of this antiquated method of locomotion were a serious hindrance to the development of these pleasant seaside villages. Few will regret even on sentimental grounds the disappearance of this relic of antiquity."

Of all the reports on the end of the Dandy, the *Aberdeen Weekly Journal's* has an eye on heritage, saying it hopes one Dandy will be preserved somewhere for posterity, being such an interesting link between modern railways and 'primitive pioneers'. The paper also describes the Dandy as being reminiscent of the old coaching days.

NBR Dandy no. 1 is preserved at the National Railway Museum, in York. No. 2 was, as Mr Reed had announced, used by the bowling and tennis club, till it deteriorated beyond repair. It is said that in 1925, the metal parts were scrapped and the woodwork sold for firewood.

But what about the people?

References to the Dandy pop up in newspapers from the *Western Daily Press* to the curiously titled *Epworth Bells, Crowle and Isle of Axholme Messenger* (both 1902) and the *Globe* (1911) – the concept of a horse-drawn carriage running on a railway line having caught the imagination of those titles.

Cumbrian papers record a couple of court cases over the years that involved passengers either fighting on board, or after alighting.

But information is thin on the drivers.

Isaac Hickson
Born about 1868, died 1831

When the Dandy made its final journey, on April 4, 1914, its driver was Isaac Hickson, who had been doing the run since at least 1901. He's also reported to have been the conductor on the first run of the new service, on April 6, 1914 – the steam-powered Sentinel railcar Flower of Yarrow.

He is one of just two Dandy drivers who both lived in Port Carlisle and were registered as such on census returns.

The 1911 census shows Isaac living at Port Carlisle, aged 43, with his wife of 21 years, Margaret Ann (née Hogg), and four of their children – Martha, aged

15, Joseph, 12, Isaac 8, and Olive, 6. The number of rooms (including the kitchen, but not counting any scullery, landing, lobby, closet, bathroom, warehouse, office, or shop) was four. Suggesting life was, as for so many families, somewhat cramped.

The census also tells us they'd had six children, but one had died. That was their first-born, Joseph William Hickson, who was born in the spring of 1891 and died three years later.

Their second-born was called Henry, after Isaac's father. He was born in 1893 and with his parents on the 1901 census, but has left home by 1911.

After Isaac and Margaret married, they initially lived with Isaac's parents, Henry and Isabella, at Drumburgh. In 1891, Isaac was a railway surfaceman and his father a retired one. There was a big gap between them: Henry was 73, Isabella was 66, their son Isaac was (a new dad at) just 21.

In 1901, when Isaac is first listed as a Dandy driver, widowed Henry was living with him and his now growing family.

Henry is said by some sources to have been a former canal pilot, who drove the first Dandy in 1857. Sadly, none of the census returns confirm this. The 1861 census records Henry as a railway labourer; 1851 has him down as an agricultural labourer, and 1841 just says 'labourer'.

That said, if whoever was driving the Dandy in 1871/881 lived in Port Carlisle, they're not accredited with it on the census.

Isaac Hickson died in 1931 – not living to see the closure of the line in May the following year. His death was deemed newsworthy because of the Dandy, with it being reported that when it stopped,

he became the first guard on its steam train replacement, continuing as a guard until he retired.

Isaac Hickson is credited in a lot of sources, with photos and postcards showing him at the reins. But what of the others who drove the Dandy?

In 1891, there is someone listed in Port Carlisle as a Dandy driver: James Wallace, a single man aged 33 who was living with his widowed mother Jane, 61.

And that's it, really. No sign of him/them before or after, and certainly not in Port Carlisle.

John Raynes
Born about 1871

Another person said to have been a driver was John Raynes, of Carlisle, who went to Drumburgh to work on the railway. A Golden Wedding report in the Cumberland News in 1949 says he'd married in Bowness on November 14, 1899, and was a native of Carlisle, attending school in Caldewgate.

The 1911 census has John Raynes, 39, married ten years to Sarah Agnes, at Westfield Bridge, Burgh-by-Sands. He's a head railway surfaceman for the NBR, born Broughton, Lancashire, and with them are three daughters, two children having died. The oldest is Agnes Mary, ten.

Sarah Agnes (née Wilson) probably wouldn't have been pleased that John got it wrong on the census (it should say 11 years), as not only had he apparently forgotten when they got married, it also falsely implied it had been a shotgun wedding, given Agnes Mary's age.

1901, Drumburgh, lists John W Raynes, 27, general labourer, born Scotland. He's with his wife Sarah A, 21, (born Bowness) and daughter Agnes M, three months.

In 1881, in Caldewgate, John is listed as being 10, born Barrow-in-Furness, and living with an uncle and aunt and their children.

William Brundrit Jefferson
Born about 1889

The only other reference I've found to a named Dandy driver was a *Cumberland News* report of the line closure. It said the last person to travel the line (in 1932) was William Brundrit Jefferson, adding that "on Saturdays he worked as relief driver on the Dandy when two coaches were required to run down to Port Carlisle".

The burials index for St Michael's, Bowness, has an entry for WB Jefferson, who died in December 1957, aged 68 (his parents, brother and sister-in-law are with him).

It was for sure a Saturday job: on the 1911 census, WB is listed as a divinity student. His father William was the rector of Kirkbride.

End of the line

The optimism of 1914 was probably always just the usual case of Port Carlisle 'hope'. But it was also a case – as usual – that it was severely dented by factors no one could have imagined. For as a wartime measure, passenger services ceased in 1917, only being reintroduced in February 1919. (The railways were brought under state control during the First World War, which continued until 1921).

Things didn't pick up when passenger services were reintroduced – not helped, perhaps, by the fact the population of Port Carlisle was small, and few people other than residents actually wanted to go there outside the summer months.

The Railways Act of 1921 aimed to stabilise the country's railways – there were more than 100, many were loss-making, and rivalries didn't help anyone. It came into force in 1923 and saw companied amalgamated into groups.

The NBR became part of the London and North Eastern Railway – the LNER. It did its best for Port Carlisle, with 'steam specials' to encourage visitors. But on May 31 (or June 1, dependent on your source), 1932, the Sentinel coach Flower of Yarrow, left Port Carlisle for Drumburgh to a 'salute' of five detonators being exploded. Its crew and ten passengers were the last to travel the line.

10

Manure

A subject not covered in any other local history book I've seen!

My Port Carlisle ancestors, between them, may have run inns and hotels, may have fished the Solway – but they were also farmers.

I'm not going to attempt to go into great detail about farming, or farming practices. Though I will mention that my grandfather – an Eden Valley farmer, who showed horses – exercised horses on the Solway sands.

It is also interesting to read the description of the tithes that farmers were paying when a survey was carried out in 1839, as part of the 1836 Tithe Commutation Act. (One of the three commissioners responsible for the Act was Cumbrian: William Blamire, who had earlier pioneered the coastal trade in Solway cattle to Liverpool).

Tithes were usually payments in kind, but could be in cash. At Port Carlisle, it is recorded:

A modus or prescription or customary payment of seven shillings and five pence is payable in lieu of the tithes or corn and grain and hay of several parcels of land called the Canal Banks extending from a place called Hurling Dub and thence in a southerly direction along the said canal to Drumburgh Marsh containing by estimation 22 acres, one rood and 29 perches, in the occupation of John Peat and of which the Carlisle Canal Company are owners.

From the family album. Farming in the late1930s

A long list of general payments in lieu for the parish includes:

For a new calved cow if milked, 3d

For a milked ewe, one farthing

For a milk goat, one penny

For a pig at 20 days, one farthing

For a fleece of wool, one half penny

For a goose, one farthing

For hens, one penny

For every cast of bees, twopence.

If it grew, mooed, flew or buzzed, you had to pay a tithe on it!

Where there's muck there's brass

But there is one part of Port Carlisle's history related to farming that may not have been covered by other authors. And it's one that may not have sat very well with the village's efforts to attract day-trippers and holidaymakers, and its boasts about the purity of the air.

Manure.

There were various forms, of course. Carlisle Cattle Market advertised manure as being one of the profits of the market; bones were another constituent; so was lime, and; guano was a valuable (if smelly) cargo for traders to import.

The Shipping Intelligence for early May 1842, for instance, details 21 vessels that had arrived at Port Carlisle (along with 19 departures), including: The Mary, (master) Irving, (from) Newry, (cargo) manure.

So great was the hype about guano, that it was deemed a news item (beyond adverts and shipping lists) when a cargo was expected – such as one at Port Carlisle in February 1845. Some experts, however, weren't taken in by 'foreign products,' proclaiming instead the virtues of Nature's natural (and effectively free) bounty – farmyard muck mixed with straw.

There were also supporters of 'animal manure – the flesh and bones of animals in a perfectly dry state, very superior to bone dust and considerably lower in price'.

Others dismissed this as inferior to Desiccated Manure (but better than Dissolved Bones). The composition of Desiccated Manure was a mix of organic matter, various phosphates, various sulphates, salts, silica, carbonate of lime, and other elements

And then there was Chemically Prepared Manure, Containing Night Soil, Bone Dust, Gypsum, Magnesia, Sulphate of Ammonia, Pearl and Soda Ash, and Coprolite.

What, beyond the fact ships carrying the stuff discharged it there, has all this to do with Port Carlisle?

Well, for one thing, you could buy it from the Victoria Warehouse at the Port. Which one hopes was downwind of, well, everything else.

In May 1854, however, a health inspector was sent to examine and report on 'a nuisance alleged to be caused by a manure depot under the railway arches leading to the Port Carlisle Station.'

I assume this was the warehouse. Manure was still being offered for sale from Port Carlisle some years later. Eg 340 tons of Odams' Patent Blood Manure, which arrived by ship in March 1859: 'stocks kept at Port Carlisle' (and elsewhere). And Lawes' Manures – 'a supply always on hand at the Victoria Warehouse, Port Carlisle' (1862)

But, it could have been from another source.

For secondly, the village had its own manure works.

Isaac Brown & Co announced in January 1854 that they had completed their works for the manufacture of peat charcoal at Port Carlisle, and could now sell powdered charcoal for manure at 50s a ton, and block charcoal to filter water for domestic purposes at 3s per hundredweight. Peat charcoal was sold for farmers to mix with farm animal excrement, or with imported guano. (The idea was it would absorb ammonia – particularly high in guano).

Isaac had been a guano merchant and seedsman until two years earlier, when he secured the right (under patent) to manufacture peat charcoal as a fertiliser.

In March 1857, the whole of the front page of the *Carlisle Journal* is given over to the National Guaranteed Manure Company, which had works at Millwall, London.

Under great detail about the company's capital, shares, aims, directors etc, Isaac Brown & Co beg to announce that they have amalgamated with the NGMC.

Farmers are told that henceforth it will be a lot cheaper to buy artificial manure (lower delivery charges), as: 'works on an extensive scale for their manufacture are now in operation at Carlisle.

The rest of the page is given over to descriptions of the products available: peat charcoal manure; crushed bones and bone dust; super-phosphates and dissolved bones, and; Brown's Concentrated Manure. Along with dozens of testimonials.

All of the above were manufactured at Carlisle. As was, from 1858, Brown's Patent Sulphuretted Carbon (patent pending).

The manures and chemicals were produced in Carlisle, but transported from there not only by rail, but also by sea (in 1859, the company had a 'free delivery within 100 miles' offer. Given the peat charcoal works there, this was no doubt via the Port.

In April 1859, the company announced the arrival at the Port of a ship bringing a large supply of bone ash, oil of vitriol, and sulphate of ammonia.

The NGMC was involved in a court case in 1859 (a dispute over a sluice in Carlisle) which set a legal benchmark. The only relevance to Port Carlisle is that it all came about from the canal having been filled in. At the Carlisle end, the water wheel that had at times pumped water from the Eden and Caldew into the canal was subsequently used to power the machinery at the manure works. This machinery ground and crushed bones and mixed manures

In 1862, the NGMC advertised its leases, plant and business goodwill for sale, by tender. The company was being voluntarily wound up (liquidated).

The list of plant etc makes it clear that Millwall was truly the smelly end of the business: it had a bone boiler, made sulphuric acid, and manufactured and stored the stuff in sheds.

The sale list for the Carlisle works included two cottages and says tramways from the Port Carlisle Railway led directly into the works.

At the Port end was the peat charcoal works, which included large charcoal ovens and machinery for grinding, worked by a steam engine. There was also the company's interest in about 100 acres of peat lands adjoining the works and licenses to cut the peat.

I've found no references to the NGMC after 1863.

While on smelly subjects...

In 1879, the Sewage Utilisation Committee of Carlisle Town Council held a lengthy meeting, discussing the proposed purchase of Willow Holme from the Duke of Devonshire, as a place to spread the city's sewage. A James Hair objected, on the grounds it would be injurious to, and a nuisance to, the health of the citizens, and the Army garrison.

He had an alternative suggestion: run pipes along the side of the Port Carlisle Railway and cast the sewage into the sea.

The town clerk asked him what the people of Port Carlisle and Bowness would think of that.

Mr Hair's unsympathetic reply was that they had the power to put the sewage into tidal water, and tidal water was where it was salt water.

The meeting ended up in confusion as to what they'd actually agreed to do (James Hair's amendment opposing the use of Willow Holme having been carried).

Another report on the situation says Mr Hair's alternative idea would cost £30,000, and result in sewage 'seesawing up and down between King Garth and Port Carlisle with every tide and never getting to the sea at all'.

The meeting was adjourned.

James Hair wasn't the only person at those meetings in favour of piping sewage to Port Carlisle.

Also present was a Mr (Dr) Reeves, who had 'form' on the subject.

Speaking at a health committee meeting some 23 years earlier, in 1856, Dr Reeves had thought then that the sea was the natural outlet. The chairman, Mr Hewson, then said while Dr Reeves had 'a partiality for Port Carlisle,' he could not support the idea.

Dr Reeves clearly had a bee in his bonnet about it, for tin 1858, as the council discussed flooding, he insisted it had been caused by the sewers. Other councillors said he'd been repeatedly told it hadn't. Mayor John Howe didn't appreciate him bringing the subject up again.

The *Carlisle Journal* reported that: "Mr Reeves (whom the mayor attempted in vain to stop) said that when Mr Rawlinson was here last, he had mentioned this to him and suggested that the sewage be carried down to Port Carlisle."

Of course, any sewage pumped or leaching into the rivers Eden, Esk, or their tributaries could find its way down into the Solway.

I'm not going to go into this subject in any greater depth. Suffice it to say sewage and the Solway is a subject that has been making headlines from the mid-19th century to this side of the millennium.

An unlikely bounty

Having listed various sources of manure, there is one more that was very much a one-off opportunity.

Port Carlisle wastewater pumping station seemed an appropriate photo!

For as anyone who has ever cleaned out a garden pond can attest, artificial bodies of water accumulate all sorts of vegetation that sinks and is turned naturally into a layer of gunge at the bottom.

Thus it was when the canal was drained, in the summer of 1853, to make way for the railway.

Carlisle, 20th October, 1853.

VALUABLE MANURE FOR SALE. TO be SOLD, to the highest bidder, the whole of the valuable MANURE deposited at the bottom of the OLD CANAL BASIN, Carlisle, has been recently drained, now the Property of the Port Carlisle Dock and Railway Company, including all articles found therein, the owners of which cannot be identified. Persons desirous of purchasing are requested to send in Tenders to Mr. William Ward, at the Company's Offices, Canal Basin, Carlisle, to endorsed Tenders for Manure, on or before Thursday, the 27th instant.

The whole of the deposit to be cleared out within Six Weeks of the Tender being accepted. The Company will not make any claim to articles that may be found.

The people

The people in this chapter are all Carlisle folk.

James Hair

There is a Scotland-born draper called James Hair, aged 54, at 13 Abbey Street on the 1871 census (with a wife and family). That would make him 62 at the time he was advocating pouring Carlisle's sewage into the Solway, to protect the health of city folk. He died in 1886.

Mr Reeves

He was referred to as either 'Dr' or 'Mr' in the council reports. There is a surgeon called William Reeves, boarding in Botchergate in 1871, aged 54. He was originally from the Isle of Man. In 1851 and 1861, he was living in Lowther Street, heading his own household with two servants. He was a freemason, and looks to have died in 1879, just weeks (at most a few months) after the council meeting.

Isaac Brown

Isaac seems to left the NGMC by the start of 1859, when the offices moved to 38 English Street. He'd listed the address previously (from at least 1853) as Bank Street. The first advert appears in 1852. There are no obvious candidates on any census.

11

The salmon saga

Salmon used to be so plentiful, servants complained at being given it to eat three days a week. From 1780, that changed

NO BOOK on the overall story of Port Carlisle would be complete without a mention of haaf-net fishing.

As I write this, it is possible for visitors to have a go, courtesy of the Highland Laddie pub at Glasson (George Carruthers' old pub in the middle of the 19th century. His first wife was Mary Peat). After a day in the water, with an experienced guide, the pub chefs will cook you a fish supper.

Today, conservation (of salmon stocks) is the key concern for the regulators – and concern that rules and limits will wreck haaf-netting is a perennial one.

Haaf-net fishing wasn't the problem in the 19th century

In the past, 'the fisheries' filled many column inches of local newspapers. Conservation was a big issue then as well. Along with who owned what bits of foreshore, and whether that meant they owned the fishing rights. And there was a big 'them and us' between the big landowners and the 'ordinary' folk who lived along the Solway coast.

How you do it

For those who don't know, haaf-netting is thought to have been introduced by the Vikings around the late

900s – 'haaf' being the Viking word for sea, or channel.

Practised for centuries in the North West, including the rivers Lune and Ribble, as well as the tributaries feeding into the Solway, the fishermen's goal is to catch salmon and sea trout.

The net is supported on a huge rectangular frame – this differs from similar fishing methods such as lave net fishing in the Severn Estuary, where the frame is Y shaped. The basic method is for the fisherman to walk out into the water and hold the net upright, facing the incoming or outgoing tide.

The net streams out in the water. Fish swim into the net and are caught.

Haaf nets are not to be confused with stake nets, which only seem to have made their appearance in the Solway from about 1780. Stake nets are erected on wooden poles set in the seabed to form a barrier which directs fish into a large pocket or trap. In 1861, a list of stake nets in the Solway shows three at Bowness which were 100 yards, 150 yards, and 300 yards long. Some on the Scottish side were 800 and 900 yards long (*see later*).

People were complaining from the 1790s that the stake nets trapped and killed fry and small fish, to the obvious detriment of fish stocks.

Poke nets, meanwhile, are secured to a row of poles set in the seabed and form a series of pockets in which the fish are caught. They pre-date stake nets considerably and seem to have been less controversial that stake nets, even though they 'inadvertently' caught salmon out of season. This was possibly because they were an accepted tradition, unlike the 'modern' stake nets; possibly because salmon stocks had only suffered after stake nets were introduced. There are also 'technical' reasons why they catch fewer fish than stake nets.

The Lowthers v everyone else

Given that wading out into the Solway is potentially very dangerous, you really need to know what you are doing.

And standing against the tide, holding steady a huge net, requires a lot of stamina, too.

Stamina is also required to wade through the seemingly endless rows over fishing in the 19th century.

You'll find some detail in the chapter on Pattinson Lawson, who collected rents – or not – for the first and second earls of Lonsdale.

And there is more detail in the chapter on Jeffray Peat (1769-1836), who was a fisherman for many years.

Peter Irving was concerned, too – though his only real contribution was to say that the Solway began after the confluence of the Esk and the Eden. Which was actually a big deal, in terms of where it was ok to set nets.

He, in 1864, was to take the side of 'the poor man' in the argument of stake nets (perceived by some to be a them/us issue between landowners and 'ordinary folk'). That division – the feeling that restrictions were there purely to benefit the landowners' river fisheries – scarcely helped conservation in the frith.

Ruler under the waves

In 1859, the case of the Earl of Lonsdale v Joseph Fell was a lengthy one. Fell claimed that custom dating from the time of Richard the Lionheart gave him the right to fish in the firth.

The earl claimed he owned all the foreshore covered at high water by the sea and no one else had any right to stake nets there.

The defence sought to prove custom and practice – that people had put stakes there all their lives, that the custom had existed the whole life of everyone living, and that everyone in the district knew of it.

It was pointed out that there was no law to stop anyone fishing from boats in the estuary (not that you could catch salmon that way), so how could it be illegal to stake nets?

A lengthy history lesson

One wonders what the jury made of one plank of evidence – a translation of *Placita de quo Warranto*, from the time of Edward I. Other than being interested to hear that Lazonby was then called Leysingby, and there were gallows in 'Burgh on Sands,' perhaps.

The relevant bit was that it set out to determine by what right, in 1292, Thomas de Multon claimed the fishing in the river Eden. Which Thomas said his ancestors had enjoyed from time immemorial. (*See the history section at the end of this chapter*).

Another document, from 1314 and the time of Edward II (it was 'Laisyngby' then, by the way), referred to raise nets and a fishery at Burgh called Polburgh, Raysdrete, and Frethnet… And on it went, with the poor jury no doubt wishing they were somewhere, anywhere else.

Shoals of thirlepolles?

What probably seemed like 'isn't it lunchtime yet?' later, the case had reached the time of Queen Elizabeth I, when there were salmon fishings called Bakkgarthe, Stokewathbedd, New Drawght, Powburgh, Freebote, and Banke End. And when any sturgeon, whale or porpoise caught technically belonged to the Crown, because they were royal fish; as were 'seales, turbettes and thirlepolles'.

Clearly, the Elizabethans didn't know the difference between fish and mammals, but maybe the jury were more puzzled, wondering what on Earth a thirlepolle was, and whether there were ever any of them in the Solway.

They certainly couldn't remember a turbot showing up.

The conclusion of the history lesson was that the lords of the Barony had some rights in the Eden – and had from time to time "come down and attacked the poor fishermen on the coast," trying to extend those rights.

A qualified victory

Mr Temple QC said that being men of poor means, the fishermen usually gave in. And that agents for the earl had been travelling down the firth for 15 years, inducing people who were not rich enough to resist to pay a small sum.

A procession of witnesses then described their experiences and knowledge, before the earl's agents said they didn't think rents had been collected between 1737 and 1843.

This case lasted three days. At the end of which the judge's comments were strongly in favour of the earl, and the jury found in his favour – possibly somewhat grudgingly, as they only granted him damages of one shilling.

The defence appealed, on the grounds the judge had misled the jury, but got nowhere.

However, in 1867, the case was to be cited as proof that Lord Lonsdale was deemed to own the foreshore, but not the fishery. Meaning he could grant a licence to stick nets in the ground, but the right to fish wasn't his to grant or decline.

Mr Mounsey told that hearing (into the legality of net types) it was clear that from all time, anyone who wanted to fish did so – it was a common law right.

Looking back

The general impression I get from the cases is that down the centuries, some landowners had sent out men to demand fishing rents; others hadn't bothered.

This may have had something to do with the type of net being used at various times, or maybe just the mood and mind of whoever was running the barony at the time.

In fact, the earl's agents were wrong about rents not being collected between 1737 and 1843, for in 1805, people living in the barony were being charged.

The Lonsdale files at Carlisle archives include: 'copy petition for access to fisheries, with copy rates of payment for fishing rights, Burgh barony, 1799-1805. It covers 'the townships or liberties' of Burgh by Sands, Rockcliffe Cross, Boustead Hill, Easton, Drumburgh, Glasson, and Cardurnock. And there are some familiar names on the lists – including Jeffray Peat, John Pattinson (Cardurnock), Joseph Askew (see the canal chapter), and a Joseph Fell – presumably a relation of the Joseph in the 1859 case.

Cruives and yairs

The 'poor fishermen' may have hated having to pay rents, but it may have had an upside if it limited the number of people putting out nets.

Back in 1804, owners of fisheries 'in the Solway Frith and rivers in England and Scotland communicating therewith' met in Dumfries, to discuss a proposed Parliamentary Bill for better regulating the fisheries. The provisions of the Act included banning nets with a mesh of less than one inch, and banning 'double-armoured nets'.

They believed the Solway Fisheries Act wouldn't solve the 'abuses' of recent years. Nothing short of banning the cruives and fish yairs that had been introduced some years ago could restore salmon

stocks that were now 'nearly exterminated'. A cruive is a wicker or wooden enclosure for catching fish; yairs were another type of fish trap, which stopped fry getting through as well as catching mature fish.

Fishing out of season was another problem that troubled the courts in the early 1800s, and harmed fish stocks.

Either stocks recovered, or what was left took a really serious hit in August 1815, when it was reported that Scottish fishermen had caught 170 salmon in one net, during one tide, in the firth between the mouths of the Esk and Sark. News the probably didn't please Solway fishermen.

A year later, it was a Carlisle magistrate and clerk of the peace who didn't appreciate the Carlisle Journal accusing them of having helped themselves to the largest of seven salmon, after convicting a man for catching them outside the permitted season. The Journal's printers were hit with a hefty bill for libel.

In May 1818, a letter writer ('X') said it was no good fining people for catching salmon in the close season if there was no moral stigma attached to doing so. Much like those people today who regard speeding tickets as 'unfair,' the writer said the present fishery Act was disdained by many. The result was widespread poaching of salmon in the close season.

Penal laws were (are) only effective when public opinion was (is) fully behind them.

A new Salmon Fishery Bill was drawn up a few months after. And X was back, worried that the small mesh of nets being used in the Solway was wrecking salmon stocks. His letter in July is long and detailed – and also includes his belief that factories along the Caldew may also be harming fish stocks.

There was a clear awareness in 1818, then, that industrial pollution was harming the natural environment. Even if no one thought you could do anything about it.

Just when you thought it was safe...

There may or may not have been thirlepolles in the Solway, but in August 1818, a man from the Scottish side called John Moffat, crossing the Esk on his way back from his salmon stake nets, was badly bitten on the leg by a five foot shark – the only case anyone could remember of one turning up in the firth.

December 1822 saw debate on a proposals to update the existing (catchily titled) *Act for better regulating and improving the Fisheries in the arm of the sea between the county of Cumberland and the counties of Dumfries and Wigton, and the Stewartry of Kirkcudbright, and also the Fisheries in the streams and waters which run into or communicate with the said arm of the sea*. There were 35 proposed clauses which, a critic pointed out, would mean different rules on the Scottish side to the English, including the length of the close season.

The clauses threatened dire punishment for offenders – but left the policing in the hands of the landowners.

And on a Sunday, too

On June 22, 1823, there were dust-ups in two places. Firstly, four 'vagabonds from Annan' tried to plunder English nets. Secondly, English 'depredators from Rockcliffe; tried to steal herring from Scottish nets. Both events led to physical struggles, but the complainant was more concerned about the fact it all took place on the Sabbath than anything else.

There was another Bill before Parliament in 1824, with a slightly shorter title – it went down like a lead balloon at a meeting of county gentlemen in Dumfries, with calls for a UK-wide Bill to be drawn up instead, to protect salmon fry and small fish, in everyone's interest.

It didn't help that no one could totally agree if small fish were small salmon or other species, nor that some muddied the waters by saying any scarcity of salmon in the frith was the fault of: (apparently voracious) porpoises; fry being killed by mill sluices, and/or; the weather.

There was also concern that fishermen would put self-interest and short-term gain ahead of the common good. This was a constant problem, referred to by many over the years.

Another was that most of the Acts were private: that is, proposed by individual politicians, for a patch that interested them, rather than by government. The Solway's position wasn't helped by it being a border between two countries: neither of which was ready to impose restrictions it couldn't also enforce the other side.

One can't help thinking a simple law on the size of nets, and the size of the mesh of nets – or rather, two identical laws, for Scotland and England – could've answered a lot of it.

The worst season yet, till the next one

The 1825 salmon season was deemed the least productive and most disastrous of a run of bad seasons, with numbers (and quality) of all species caught well down... until 1827 (year of yet another fisheries Bill, which was shredded at committee stage and withdrawn). For the 1827 salmon season was 'the worst within the memory of man'.

1828: a new season, a new fisheries Bill. But two years later, fishermen were still catching anything that swam in stake nets in season, and poachers were still catching salmon out of season. Leading to… 1832 being 'unusually unproductive'. Suggesting 'worse than ever', given that there was sadly nothing unusual about a poor season. Someone killed a whale in the Solway that year, but there's no mention of thirlepolles.

A hefty haaf-net

A court case in November accused David James of Glasson of catching salmon in the close season (*see the chapter on Jeffray Peat, who was a witness*).

In 1833, a court action was pending in relation to the fisheries. It would determine if the the several hundred families who supplied local markets with flounders and other fish should be allowed to continue to do so. The prosecution case was that the nets were illegal. Another legal action was going through over the destruction (by cutting) of nets in the Eden. But experts still couldn't agree if certain small fish were or were not young salmon – and lawyers were still arguing in 1836 where exactly the Solway began.

Pellochs and bullets

There was another Bill, more arguments, and more gloom: neither 1837 nor 1840 were good years for salmon. But suddenly, in 1841, every kind of fish in the Solway was more abundant than in previous years. They had a 'new' enemy, though. While a school of 40 porpoises were hailed as 'playful' and a sign that herring were plentiful in 1842, 'greedy pollochs' were reported to be taking lumps out the

salmon and trout in the rivers. (In 1857, they were 'pellochs', in a report on how a fisherman on the Scottish side of the Solway had, with his dog, killed a raccoon he found devouring the fish in his nets).

Things turned nasty that Christmas. A party of fishery proprietors (or their agents) set out to destroy nets that had been set illegally – and were shot at, from Glasson. They returned fire, which ended things. Luckily, no one seems to have been hurt.

Friend of the poor, defender of the oppressed

That was the flattering description of the *Carlisle Journal* used by a letter writer in 1843, seeking support for the Bowness parish tenants.

If you've kept awake this far in this chapter, you'll recall the (1859) suggestion that no fishing rents had been collected from 1737-1843.

Lord Lonsdale was now (1843) claiming tenants had to pay for 'breaking the soil' (ie sticking nets in it). The writer claimed Sir John Lowther in 1687 had granted tenants the right to enjoy a whole bunch of things, including the fisheries, in return for him tripling their (trifling) ancient customary rent.

The letter writer, bursting with indignation, implies the present lord was out to extend his dominions by wrenching rights from the poor and unprotected, from people who kept their families off the parish (welfare relief) by fishing.

The fishermen had been told they must pay half a sovereign a year per trap net. And four men with hatchets stood by, ready to destroy the nets if they refused. They paid up, thus (reluctantly) setting a legal precedent (an admission rents were payable).

At least the fish stocks were more plentiful, in 1845, than they had been for many years. There was a new fisheries Bill a year later, which included a clause barring fixed nets, and nets under a certain-sized mesh – but the Solway was excluded from its provisions.

Let's fast-forward

By now, unless you are really, really fascinated, it's all starting to seem a bit same-y.

So. let's jump forward to March 1877, and a Hansard report (and then back to 1860).

Sir Edward Stafford Howard called for a royal commission to be set up, to look at stake nets in the Solway and the "injustice consequent upon the conflicting state and interpretation of the laws affecting the Solway Fisheries in England and Scotland."

He was cheered by local fishermen who met at the Steam Packet to back him and to object to the said injustice. Stafford Howard was a Liberal MP for Cumberland East, and part of the Greystoke Castle Howard dynasty.

He likened the various Acts as like putting together a Chinese puzzle. From 1804 to 1861, the Solway was under one uniform law. But about 1860, UK salmon fisheries had so deteriorated—owing, he believed, chiefly to stake nets—that a committee of the House of Lords was appointed to inquire into the subject as to Scotland, and a Royal Commission in respect of England. Both agreed that 'fixed engines' (stake nets) should be banned or heavily regulated.

The Royal Commission visited (among other places) Carlisle in October 1860, followed by Workington – the hearings filled many, many column inches in the local press.

The *Carlisle Journal* thought the whole thing should be simple: stake nets were to blame for a drop in fish stocks since the 1780s, and should be banned. And everyone with an interest, be it in the sea or the rivers, should pull together in the common good, rather than indulging in short-term greed and self-interest, with no care for the future.

The Commission duly produced a book of '545 closely printed pages' and a 36-page report. Key recommendations were: a central board to control and mediate between the various interests, and; the banning of all 'fixed engines' (stake and poke nets).

The English Act banned stake nets. The Scottish one was supposed to have done so – but the ban didn't have to come into force until two years after it was applied on the English side.

That actually didn't advantage the Scottish fishermen quite as much as it might: there were reports in 1862 of boatloads of Lancastrians crossing over from Silloth to stake nets the other side.

The inequality of Scotland 'bristling with stake nets' persisted long after, hence the 1877 fuss.

If anyone is that interested in the whole of that story, set aside a LOT of time. And then a lot more time to cover things from 1877 to the present day.

'Stake nets are fixed into the ground on parts of the Solway coast. At right angles to the shore, they cover several hundred yards and a number of traps are set into the lines of the net.' The quote is from a BBC story about stake nets being banned near Annan, to help fish stocks… in 2015.

Interested parties

So far, the only Port Carlisle folk mentioned in this chapter have been been referred to with 'see chapter on… for more detail'.

But, in 1867, Special Commissioners were appointed to look into the legality all fixed nets and engines used for the capture of salmon. Their seven-day hearing, in Carlisle, heard from more than 50 witnesses, many of them from Port Carlisle, Bowness, and surrounds.

Claims were made, overall, for upwards of 7,000 poke nets to be declared legal, along with 1,500 stream nets, and (Lord Lonsdale) four raise nets.

The Carlisle Journal described the proceedings as 'tedious and uninteresting in some respects'! However, the Journal said they had shone light on the various destructive means used to catch fish, and on the fact pretty much everyone in the Bowness area reckoned they had the right to set nets as they liked.

At issue was whether poke nets were legal. The fishermen (and Lord Lonsdale, through his agent) argued various reasons why they should be allowed to set nets.

The arguments against were:

1. the lord of the manor had never owned the fishery, so had never had any right to let it out,

2. the only right under which poke nets had been used was the common law right of all the Queen's subjects to fish in tidal waters, and that would not legalise engines fixed in the soil.

3. a survey in the time of Elizabeth I mentioned one raise net. Singular.

4. as it was a tidal river, nets could interfere with navigation, so there had never been any right to use fixed nets.

I'm not going to list the individuals' net lengths, nor all the witnesses, but will stick to a few people who feature elsewhere in this book, and other Port Carlisle residents.

John Topping
Born circa 1800, died 1878

John said he was a proprietor in Bowness, and had fished himself, as had his father before him. He'd fished circa 1857-61, with poke nets. The property he referred to was his wife's: her father had fished. He'd lived with his father till he farmed the property.

John was a stonemason prior to his marriage to widowed Isabella Irving in 1830. She was the daughter of Joseph Lawson, and sister of Jane Lawson who married (Peter's brother) James Irving. I've not found a first marriage for Isabella.

On the 1841 census, John, stonemason, is followed by Isabella, 40; Lawson, 10; Christopher, 6; Judith, 2; and Mary, 2. Chris and Judith look to have been named after his parents. Only Lawson isn't with them ten years later, when step-daughter Margaret Irving, 25 (born Liverpool) is. John Topping died in Port Carlisle

Jeffrey Peat

Born 1833, died 1912

Jeffrey was the son of John and Elizabeth, who has her own chapter. Jeff told the 1867 hearing that he rented and occupied a field owned by John Will which fronted the Solway. He'd fished for 20 years with the poke net and stream net — ten years of it before occupying JW's land. (I think from the evidence he'd been fishing for ten years from land he didn't own/rent!). He'd never used trap nets.

He said there were more fishermen now than before the trap nets were put down, that people had come from a distance. If proprietors could prove their right, and if interlopers were stopped, it would improve the fishing in the district. He caught flounders in the stream nets, sometimes cod, and sea ---- an odd time (laughter). Any whales? Yes (laughter). Any salmon? Very seldom (laughter).

He also said he'd never heard it that fishing was confined to those who had property: he had heard his father (John) say it was confined to those who had houses.

Jeff never married, but provided a home for assorted family members when he moved to the White Ox (as a publican and farmer) at High Hesket, in the 1870s. He also became a district councillor there.

Thomas Peat

Born 1834, died 1881

Thomas was Jeff's brother. He told the 1867 inquiry Jeff had occupied a field, from 1857-1864, belonging to Mr Hodgson, and fished with poke nets. He (Jeff) had fished before occupying that field and since. He remembered Thomas Simpson (that could be his grandfather, or his uncle) fishing, but could not say what. He thought 'all the people down there' had a right to fish, and still would, too (laughter). He was

told the hearing wasn't about IF people should fish, but the method.

He didn't marry, either – but he did have an illegitimate daughter, Mary Ann Coulthard, born in 1871, who he named in his will. Her mother was Jane Coulthard, from Stanwix. It's not hard to work out the story: the 1871 census shows the Peats, including Thomas, living at Kirkland House. Jane, aged 25, is there too, as a general servant.

Peter Irving (see his chapter)

Peter claimed a poke net on behalf of Thomas Simpson (presumably his nephew, who was a Bowness farmer), for whom he was trustee. The property in right of which was claimed consisted of five dwelling houses. Mr Simpson used a poke net through his tenant Joseph Faulder between 1857-61, and then on his own account.

Joseph Faulder

Born circa 1803, died 1872 (unconfirmed)

Joseph said he was now the tenant of Jane Powell (no location) and fished as he had done when he lived at Port Carlisle. In 1871, he was listed as a fisherman on the census, living at Port Carlisle with his wife 'Philles', 63. He was born Holme Cultram, she was née Tordiff, and born Castle Sowerby. In 1861, they were living at Glasson, with Joseph listed as a fisherman.

John Faulder

Born circa 1830

John F said he lived at Port Carlisle, on his father's property: they were Mr Toppin's tenants*. He'd lived there seven or eight years (and previously at Bowness and Glasson). He is on the 1861 census with his parents at Glasson, so in fact, it would have been six years at most. He wasn't there in 1871.

He'd fished for 15 years, no matter where he lived. He used poke nets and it made no difference to him where he fished. Asked if it was the practice for anyone who lived at Port Carlisle to fish, he said he was shoemaker as well as a fisherman.

(*Joseph Toppin then explained he was trustee of Mrs Powell's property).

William Thompson
Born about 1808, died 1894 (unconfirmed)

A Port Carlisle blacksmith, William said he had lived there 24 years and rented a house of Mrs (Elizabeth) Peat. He used a poke net and stream net.

In 1861, he had a wife (Isabella) and four children, all four born in Port Carlisle. He and Isabella were still living in Port Carlisle in 1881, moving along to Bowness between then and 1891.

Peter Brough
Born about 1812

PB told the hearing he'd lived in Port Carlisle for 20 years, and owned a house. He'd fished there with poke nets, stream nets, trap nets and all. The land on which his property was built was freehold and he paid no customary rent to Lord Lonsdale.

He set his nets between the Port and Bowness. He'd lived at Bowness for 25 years and fished a long time there.

Peter was the son of Robert, who is mentioned in the chapter on Jeffray Peat (b 1769). In 1841, he was with his parents at Bowness, a stonemason. In 1851, he was at Port Carlisle, with wife Mary (née Bell), daughters Mary, Elizabeth and Jane, and a servant. His occupation is listed as 'house houlder bilder' (sic). He's still there in 1861, with Mary, Jane, and another daughter, Margaret, 8 (who looks to have died aged just 14). The older daughters are elsewhere. By 1871, it's just him, still in Port Carlisle, his wife Mary having died – possibly in 1866.

William Murray junior
Born 1833

WM said he'd lived at Port Carlisle all his life, with his father, and had always fished with poke nets and stream nets. His father, who had also fished before him, rented the house of David Irving (Peter's brother) and he'd been there five or six years. It hadn't made any difference to his fishing where he lived.

"All the people of Port Carlisle fish as they like, I believe."

The 1861 census shows William as a labourer, living with his parents, William and Fanny, and sister Margaret. Twenty years earlier, William senior had been the Port Carlisle lock-keeper.

John Pattinson, of Westfield House (*see separate chapter*) said he had 'always fished' – from when he lived at Cardurnock to now. Westfield House was owned by Ann Pattinson (sic), whose late husband Jeremiah Sharp had fished all his life.

Jeremiah's son John Sharp said he had about 100 yards of net, about the same as his late father, who had fished at Glasson (poke nets) long before he went to Westfield.

By now, the commissioners must have been starting to yawn, for it was suggested the rest of the witnesses limit themselves only to their names and the number of yards of net for which they claimed.

This they did, although William Witherington (a farm servant), and Jacob Greenwood (a joiner) said they lived at Port Carlisle. While various local landowners gave evidence of where they fished, and how. William was born about 1813, at Bowness. Jacob was born about 1820 in Caldbeck. Both were living in Port Carlisle in 1871, Jacob with a wife and seven children.

The conclusion

The commissioners decided (in May 1867) that all the poke nets, trap nets and raise nets were illegal and must be removed. Likewise the stream nets.

They said Lord Lonsdale had the right to one raise net, but that right had lapsed because it hadn't been exercised between 1857-61.

In consideration of the large number of persons dependent on these means of fishing, the order would not be imposed till the end of the season.

The Commission was still waiting for the Home Secretary to decide if they had jurisdiction in Scotland.

One implication of all this was that the Lowthers had never had any right to charge fishing rents. Presumably the counter to that was 'we were charging for use of the beach, not for fishing'. It's no surprise that his lordship (along with a handful of others, including Ann Pattinson) appealed the ruling.

The Bowness (etc) men just quietly removed their nets at the end of the season.

It didn't end there, of course. There were appeals, the unfair disparity with Scotland continued, the 'poor fishermen' put the nets back up, illegally, a year later (police removed 547 of them in May 1868).

But I think 5,300 words is plenty for what is just one

section of this book.

Autumn 1860 stake nets

Raven Bank		
Net	Chambers	Length (arm yards long)
1	1	40
1	2	170

Bowness		
Net	Chambers	Length (arm yards long)
1	1	150
1	2	100
1	5	300

Cardurnock		
Net	Chambers	Length (arm yards long)
1	3	200

Skinburness		
Net	Chambers	Length (arm yards long)
1	1	80
1	1	80
1	1	40
1	1	60
1	1	60
1	1	100
1	2	100
1	1	120
1	2	140
1	1	100
1	2	200

Kirtlepoint		
Net	Chambers	Length (arm yards long)
1	2	250
1	2	300
1	2	300
1	1	300
1	4	140
1	2	400
1	2	100
1	5	400
1	5	600
1	1	600
1	4	80
1	5	900
1	5	900
1	6	800
1	3	800
1	1	200
1	1	120

Newby		
Net	Chambers	Length (arm yards long)
1	1	80
1	3	200
1	1	100
1	2	80
1	3	150
1	1	100
1	4	300
1	1	150
1	10	1000
1	1	100
1	1	100
1	1	100

And here's the history

THE BARONY of Burgh is first found in history as the property of Robert de Trivers, or d'Estrivers (according to an historian in 1855). Barons used to divide their property into manors, and hand those out to lords, in return for their service in arms.

Bowness (Bulness) 'at that time a wild waste,' was assigned (with Drumburgh as its HQ) to Gamel le Brun. Who may not have been a Norman, given the 'Gamel' isn't a Norman name. The manor passed down the le Brun line, with the family also known by an alternative name, de la Feritate.

Some claim Drumburgh = bitterns' fen. It's far more likely to come from 'droim' (Celtic for 'ridge'), ('burgh' being a fortified place, rather than a town, surely?). It was the burgh on the hill, as against burgh on the sands.

And then it gets confusing

Version A
A succession of daughters (no male heirs), saw it change families by marriage a few times, to the Engains, then the Morvilles, then to the Moultons of Gilsand in the early 1200s).

After the Moultons, it fell by marriage again (from the early 14th century) to the Dacres. When George Lord Dacre died in 1569, the barony passed to his sister Anne Howard, wife of Phillip, the earl of Arundel. Henry Howard, the seventh duke of Norfolk, sold it to Sir John Lowther in 1685 – no idea if he gave his Greystoke cousins first dibs…

Version B
However, another source has '1342, Richard Brun, Lord of Drumburgh'. And a third source says the barony was split between female heiresses and the last male le Brun in the reign of Richard II (king from 1377-1399), with the Dacres later buying up the shares to reunite the barony. Thomas Lord Dacre rebuilt Drumburgh Castle in the reign of Henry VIII. And in 1678, Henry Howard sold it and the demesnes round it to John Aglionby. Who did it up, before swapping it with Sir John Lowther for Nunnery.

Whatever the history of the barony, quite simply there was nothing at Port Carlisle till someone built Kirkland House and the old Binnacle.

Except everyone says it was called Fisher's Cross. Though Fiza's Cross was deemed an alternative circa 1800. Was 'fiza' an old word for 'fisherman'? Or a person?

A sketch map of the moss, from the 1600s, shows (hard to read): - - - of Kirkland; Hurling-dub; Baghall - - -; and something illegible as the only things between Drumburgh and Bowness. Baghall being about where Hesket House is (very roughly – it's hardly to scale).

12

This and that

During the course of my research, I came across all sorts of human interest stories that didn't fit the main chapters of this book.

So, here are some of them.

Brandy for the parson, 'baccy for the clerk

Like anywhere else with a coast, the Solway was popular with smugglers. A fact I first realised when going through the Bowness parish registers and spotting references to smugglers among the burials.

Other people have written whole books on the subject, so I'm not going to cover it at any length. But here's one story that has a follow-up.

In September 1857, the master of a ship called the Nestor and his son were up on court, accused of smuggling tobacco.

James Barnes, the principal coast officer at Port Carlisle, had boarded the Nestor at Port Carlisle before it landed. On board, he found some buckets in the captain's state room. They were packed inside one another, and in the last bucket he found a parcel containing six pounds of tobacco. The master of the ship, Capt Stewart, said he knew nothing about it. His son John said the tobacco was his.

The family of young smuggler Thomas Stoal, from the Isle of Man, had this gravestone erected at Bowness. He died in 1755

As John was deemed to be unaware of the serious nature of the offence, the court imposed the value of the tobacco (12s); the import duties (£2 16s 9d), and: costs, 14s 4d.

It's hardly *Jamaica Inn*! The interest is that I chanced up on an item about the Nestor two months later.

84

Wreck of the Nestor: On October 28, the brig went down at the north point of Prince Edward's Island, in a gale, thick fog, and sleet.

She'd been on her way from her home port of Carlisle to fetch a cargo of timber for R Creighton, of Carlisle. The only cargo on board when she was wrecked was coal.

The whole crew was saved, including Captain John Stewart.

The Nestor was advertised in a Liverpool paper in 1844 as being two years old and ready to sail to Montreal under the experienced command of Captain William Stewart. Coincidence? She seems to have other captains before 1857, and was advertised for sale in 1847 – which may explain how she went from being a Liverpool vessel to a Port Carlisle one.

Meanwhile, a Captain Stewart was master of Peter Irving's brig Robert Burns at times in the early 1850s.

'Nestor, (captain) Stewart' first appears in shipping intelligence in January 1856. She left Port Carlisle on what turned out to be her last voyage on October 17, 1857, for Miramichi, New Brunswick.

She was partly insured. Most of the shareholders lived in or around Carlisle.

There's a master mariner called John Stewart living in Port Carlisle in 1851, with his wife Jane, four children, and a domestic servant. Son John – the bucket smuggler (as it were) of 1857 – was then aged ten. John senior was born in Dumfries in 1811, Jane in Bowness, the children all in Liverpool, reflecting the life of a mariner's family. Jane and the children were there in 1841 (he was no doubt away at sea). And he and Jane were back there by 1861.

If son John is 'immortalised' by stuffing tobacco into a bucket, another son James, at 19 (in 1856) is forever recorded as having been admitted to the Dreadnought Seamen's Hospital in 1856, aged 19, with VD.

Another son, Joseph, shows up aged 30 on the 1871 census on board a ship called Onieza, docked in Cardiff. He was the chief officer.

Captain John Stewart was master of Peter Irving's brig the Robert Burns from 1851-55. He died in Havana, Cuba, in 1862, while master of the Mary Adelia. He had married Jane Irving at St Michael's, Bowness, on November 11, 1835.

I believe she was Peter Irving's sister. A connection I only uncovered from digging into the story of the buckets on board the Nestor!

'Youth will have its fling'

In the chapter on Peat twins, I've described how they both married three times, the second time (at least) possibly out of economic necessity. I hope this story from 1876 was one of love and companionship.

On Tuesday July 4, at Wigton Register Office, John Glaister married Ann Sharp. Their combined age was 140 and both had been married twice before.

They arrived back at Port Carlisle by the 7pm train, where they were received by a salute of tin cans from a number of children. This sounds like a variation on today's custom of tying tin cans to the exhaust of the car that takes the bride and groom off after the celebrations.

Happily, John and Ann were still in Port Carlisle in 1881, when they are both listed as 72 and born (only) Cumberland. He was a stone mason.

Ann is not Ann Sanderson who married 1 John Pattinson and 2 Jeremiah Sharp – she died in 1873.

Weather the storm

I've touched briefly in the chapter on the canal on problems posed by the weather: 1826 wasn't the only year it froze (1841, for instance). Lack of wind was often a problem for shipping that needed to get up as far as Port Carlisle.

A list of weather reports would not be especially illuminating, but it's worth giving a flavour of conditions that could be experienced at the Port.

Tides on January 7, 1839; and February 26 and November 9, 1842; were so high as to be deemed newsworthy. The Port was lucky, though: the 1839 hurricane cause devastation elsewhere, and became a benchmark (comparison) for storms for decades after.

The steamer Royal Victoria, from Port Carlisle, hit a dreadful storm in January 1843, losing 80 sheep and four cattle washed overboard.

Citizens in Carlisle spent part of Christmas 1852 in their cellars, as a gale shook buildings 'like an earthquake'. Slates, chimney pots, bricks and coping

stones were hurled about, and a woollen mill at Willow Holme was flattened.

The gales destroyed most of the outer pier at Maryport, and the iron lighthouse. At Workington, the old part of the Merchant's Quay gave way from the force of the waves, and the new part soon followed.

The tide at Port Carlisle, which should have been 16 feet, was blown up to 26 feet and two vessels broke their moorings (but weren't damaged). The Port itself escaped with 'minor injury' to the jetty.

In 1858, residents were reported to have been scared in the night by a terrible storm. The wind blew from the south-west, right up the Solway, in the worst storm anyone had witnessed in 20 years (or possibly six!)

Near 'Knox's Cross', between Port Carlisle and Bowness, a huge mound of shingle was thrown up on the road – 450 cart-loads of the stuff. While at the lower end of the village (Port Carlisle or Bowness?), the tide flowed up beneath the windows of a house.

No damage of any importance was done.

Let the train take the strain

In 1761, a relative of mine, Dr John Wasdale, made minor history when he rode 300 miles from Carlisle to London in 28 hours, taking 30 for the return journey five days later.

For most people, however, the journey to London would have been undertaken by stagecoach. In February 1777, a new post coach from Carlisle to London was announced. Travelling via Ripon, Harrowgate, Leeds and Sheffield, it took three days to reach the capital.

In 1838, it was announced with excitement that thanks to the railways, you could now reach London in just over a day – if you went via Port Carlisle.

Passengers had to get to the Port by 5pm, and catch a steamer to Liverpool. From there, they could catch a train at 6.30am, arriving in Birmingham at 11am. They could then lunch somewhere, before catching the 1pm train to London, arriving just after 8pm.

Short-changing customers

Port Carlisle was hardly a hot-bed of crime, beyond the occasional drunken fight – and the odd case of publicans serving drink outside licensing hours. There is a gravestone at St Michael's for two women who were 'cruelly murdered,' but they lived at Bromfield.

Another crime was shop-keepers, knowingly or not, cheating the customers with short measures.In September 1859, two Glasson grocers, George Carruthers and Joseph Miller, were each fined 5s plus around 11s costs for using light weights. Drumburgh innkeepers were fined for giving short measure. And at Port Carlisle, Elizabeth Rome and Mary Wilson were each fined 2s 6d plus 7s 6d costs, again for light weights. Mary's defence was that she didn't use the weights for selling in the shop, but for weighing flour when she baked bread.

The bench reprimanded all the defendants, saying it was great shame the poor were deprived of proper weight after paying the full amount for their goods.

Entertainment

Having grown up in a village, the community events of the 1900s don't seem dissimilar enough to warrant covering. My childhood years were punctuated by events such as the WI produce show, the church fête, the summer sports day, the village bonfire and fireworks...

The Barony of Burgh had a gala day to look forward to in summer, with races and wrestling.

In July 1851, a good day's sport was expected, on the course near Knock Cross. The Burgh Barony Plate (horse race) was causing a lot of speculation and interest, with a purse of £7 to be wrestled for. Gala day didn't just appeal to local folk – the Arrow (boat) was all set to carry spectators to the Port from Carlisle.

A year earlier, crowds of maybe 3,000, came from as far as Manchester, Newcastle, and London, to witness a road race between two contestants, from Port Carlisle to Burgh.

John Syddell, of Manchester faced George Hope, of Coathill – with the betting odds heavily in favour of the Lancastrian.

I've included it because Hope is such a theme of this book. However, just as so many other high hopes came to nothing, George was out-paced. After just 100 yards, he had fallen three yards behind Syddell. Syddell gradually increased his lead, winning by about 100 yards.

As a final tale: it was hardly official entertainment, but the spectacle must have provided some. On September 21, 1859, nine of the Carlisle Corporation's 15 swans decided to have a day trip out of the city. They paddled down the river to Port Carlisle – from where they were taken back to the city by two policemen in a horse and cart.

13

Peter Irving

Many of the pivotal figures in Port Carlisle's history were city men. But one key man not only had business interests in the Port, he lived there

**Born about 1804 Bowness,
died January 26, 1869, Port Carlisle**

Peter Irving was a shipowner and merchant and a key figure in Port Carlisle's economy. He was also part of a family that can trace its roots back to around 1450, the presumed birth year of Christopher Irving, Laird of Bonshaw, who led the Scottish Light Horse at the Battle of Flodden in 1513, where he was killed.

Fast-forward a few generations and William Irving (circa 1690 to circa 1775) was an active Jacobite in 1715 and 1745.

A detail from the grave at Bowness

It was William's son Joseph (born circa 1732, Kirkbean, Scotland) who became the first mariner/merchant/ship owner of the family.

Joseph's siblings included: James, another well-known Jacobite; Thomas, a colonial civil servant and counter-revolutionary, and; Charles, a naval doctor who demonstrated a method for the desalination of sea water.

It was Joseph's son James Irving (born about 1776) who crossed the Solway in terms of residence. James married Margaret Hodgson on May 27, 1799, at St Michael's Church, Bowness-on-Solway. James was a sea captain.

Of James' and Margaret's children, four were to follow their father to sea: James (b 1802); Peter (b about 1804); Richard (b 1808), and David (born 1812).

Born and married at Bowness

Peter was their second son. He was born at Bowness, and also married there, the date being May 23, 1831, and his bride Jane Simpson (1807-1890), daughter of a yeoman farmer, Thomas Simpson (who in 1818 bought one £50 share in the Carlisle Canal). Jane's sister Elizabeth married John Peat.

Years later, Peter gave information in a fishing inquiry saying (if you do the maths!) he'd lived at Port Carlisle from 1835.

The baptism records of his first four children (1832-36) list him as a mariner, of Bowness.

Three of those children were to make it to adulthood, but the second, Margaret, died aged 20 (*see the chapter on PJ Irving*). And the Irvings suffered a terrible 'run': the next five children all died under the age of two, and the next (their tenth of 12) died aged 7.

By the time son Peter John was baptised, in June 1849, Peter was being described as a merchant.

I've not found specific reference to him before 1834, although newspapers before that time have plenty of listings for sailings of vessels to and from Port Carlisle. The name Irving appears as master sometimes, but with no first name or initial, it tells us little as the surname is not uncommon. And of course, some of the references would have been one or other of his brothers or other family members.

The 1834 reference is to Peter being one of two stewards for the annual hunt, with the hounds to leave Port Carlisle at 7am, from Mrs Thwaites' Solway Hotel.

In fact, the 1841 census for Port Carlisle lists Peter's occupation as 'farmer'. He is there with his wife Jane, children Thomas, Margaret, James and Rachel.

And the tithe map (from 1839) shows that as well as renting a house almost opposite the canal basin, he occupied a strip of land of about 26 acres, running back from the shoreline, a short way past The Binnacle.

(Peter's mother Margaret owned and occupied a house and had around three acres of land at Bowness. A list of ships and their owners from 1840 also includes 'Margaret Irving and others). (*See the tables of ships*).

However, 26 acres of arable land wasn't going to make his fortune (as a comparison, his father-in-law, Thomas Simpson, farmed 134 acres).

A notice advertising the auction of the schooner Friends, of Carlisle appeared in the *Carlisle Journal* in February (before the census was taken). It was actually for one fourth share of the schooner, triggered by the death of a William Bowman. The 40-ton coastal trader was lying at Port Carlisle. Further particulars were to be had from a Mr Weir, or Mr. Jonathan Bowman, Carlisle; Mr. Peter Irving, Port Carlisle; Mr. David Baxter, Annan; or to the Captain on Board.

Brothers with talents

Peter Irving's older brother James was, as already mentions, also a sea captain. In October 1840, he was the commander of the 300-ton City of Carlisle. Owned by the Carlisle, Annan, and Liverpool Steam Navigation Company, she sailed between Port Carlisle and Liverpool.

The two brothers were clearly regarded as experts in their field. In August 1841, the brig Samuel Kelly capsized on Red Sands, near Bowness, while carrying timber from Quebec to Port Carlisle. The Crew took to a jolly boat and the Solway steamer picked them up. The brig righted on evening tide and was towed up to the new wall.

A month later, she was surveyed by Lloyds, at Port Carlisle, and the repairs passed as ok. The survey was done by an agent for Lloyds, Captains James and Peter Irving, and George Mandell, ship carpenter.

The brothers had other talents up their sleeves as well. The Loyal Northern Solway Lodge of the Oddfellows held a parade in 1842 from Port Carlisle to Bowness for a church service, then back to the Solway Hotel and dinner for 100. The toasts for some reason included the board and directors of Manchester United. It was reported that the evening was enlivened 'by some excellent songs from Messrs Irving' (and four others).

Later that year, Peter Irving was a trustee (one of three) sorting the affairs of Jonathan Bowman, draper and hatter, of Carlisle, for his creditors. Presumably the Jonathan Bowman who, with Peter, owned a quarter share of the schooner Friends. The official notice describes Peter as a ship owner.

This happy times of the Oddfellows evening were not to be repeated. James Irving died suddenly, aged 40, on March 22, 1843, in Newry, Ireland. The death notice says he was the master of the brig Jane, of Carlisle, and had seemed to be in good health. He'd written to a friend in the morning in good spirits, but soon after, working at the windlass, fell and almost instantly died. He was 'a man much-respected by his employers and all who knew him'.

There are other references to Peter in the following years, but the next of real interest is that he was one of four men appointed as constables for Bowness-on-Solway in 1848.

A real-life Onedin Line!

The North of England Civic Trust has online a fine painting of the sailing brig Robert Burns, moored at Port Carlisle in 1860. She sailed regularly from Port Carlisle to Quebec, with space for up to 40 passengers, and from 1849, adverts for the sailings advised passengers to apply to any of four people, including Peter Irving of Port Carlisle.

If like me you've watched The Onedin Line (the 1970s TV series being shown in 2018 on the Drama channel), you'll have an idea of what it was like to be a ship owner in Victorian times. It's tempting to imagine Peter Irving's life being similar! For sure, there were dramas.

One of these involved an apprentice called William Smith, who for whatever reason, in 1849, ran away from his master. At Carlisle Court House, he was sentenced to be imprisoned for a month.

As the constable took him from the dock, Smith told Peter to 'mind his eyes' and that he would be the death of him when be came out.

The magistrates dealt with the threat by telling Smith that when he came out of prison, he must find sureties to keep the peace for 12 mouths. It would seem Smith couldn't, as a month later, 'being unable to find bail, he was committed to prison'.

Smith may have got the message, as that seems to be the end of him troubling Peter. But there is a reminder not long after that seafaring was a dangerous occupation. For Peter helped examine, as being correct, sums paid out by the Merchant Seamen's Fund of the Port of Carlisle to widows and dependents.

His support for those in need was also expressed in his continued support of the Oddfellows – he was the vice-chairman of the lodge in 1850. And also in his failed attempt to be elected, in 1851, as a poor law guardian

The Carlisle Patriot reported that the election had 'caused no little excitement (almost equivalent to a county election)'. Robert Pattinson, of Whitrigg, and Pattinson Lawson, of Bowness Hall kept their posts (*see also the chapter on PL*). Peter Irving and a John Watson of Easton were 3rd and 4th.

In the census that year, Peter's entry reads: farmer 21 acres, ship owner, slate and coal merchant, fish ?cure, employing one farm servant and one cooper, and a domestic servant. As well as his wife and four of their children, they were playing host to a shipwright and his wife, and to an apprentice. Hopefully one who was happier in the job than William Smith had been.

Port Carlisle versus the west coast

For all Peter's adult life until now, Port Carlisle had been served by the Carlisle Canal. But, as I've covered in my chapter on the canal, things had been going from bad to worse for some years. Not helped by Lord Lonsdale's Raven Bank Jetty, erected in 1844, which had caused the harbour to clog up with sand, which by 1849 prevented large steamers and timber ships from using the port. It wasn't demolished until 1851, by which time even vessels of modest draught were struggling or unable to get into Port Carlisle harbour.

In 1852, it was agreed to convert the canal into a railway. And that went down like a lead balloon with supporters of the Maryport and Carlisle Railway, and the west-coast ports.

A lot of people were keen to share their opinions, via the local press, but as many of them used pen names to do so, one can only guess as to their motives.

A letter in the *Carlisle Patriot* on January 8, 1853, was signed 'Master Mariner' and dated Maryport. He was responding to the canal committee's

Master Mariner's letter says the problem is neither the canal nor the proposed railway, but the Solway. He claims sailing vessels can only enter or leave Port Carlisle at high tide and in a fair wind. He also claims underwriters charge higher premiums for ships going up the Solway (as 'proof' of navigation issues). And praises Maryport.

Peter jumped to defend Port Carlisle, sending a long letter to the Patriot, based on 'thirty years' experience in the Solway Frith'.

He rebuts each of Master Mariner's arguments, saying: "I believe he knows much about the Solway he does about the moon."

As well as defending Port Carlisle and the Solway, Peter gets in a few digs about Maryport, including suggesting people compare the damage done to shipping at Port Carlisle and at Maryport in December's gales, before judging for themselves.

Peter's letter met with a long, sarcastic response from the still anonymous A Master Mariner. 'Peter leaves us to infer he is a GREAT shipowner of extensive maritime experience and a scientific navigator of the seas...' Peter may have 'exalted notions' and 'may have come down occasionally in moderate weather with a scarce wind'. Before accusing him of regarding the losses at Maryport in the gales 'with levity' and 'apparent satisfaction'.

He asks if Peter expects to be Port Carlisle's harbour master if the railway Bill passes, saying if so, 'the Port will doubtless become another Liverpool under his superintendence'.

And after saying he won't trouble himself to respond to anything else Peter might say, says he 'fearlessly' leaves the matter to be adjudged by their 'seafaring friends'.

Peter may have decided it wasn't worth a slanging match, although other letters on the topic follow, such as that from A Bone Fide Shareholder in the Maryport and Carlisle Railway, who concedes the interests of his railway are 'antagonistic' with those of the canal/Port Carlisle railway. A pro-Port Carlisle letter-writer refers to another as 'another of the Maryport breed'.

Meanwhile, one leading light of the (neutral!) Newcastle and Carlisle Railway believed the water was as good at Port Carlisle as at Maryport; while another believed Maryport had the same obstruction problems (sand) as Port Carlisle – and they'd be better off using Whitehaven!

A fight over herrings

Peter soon had other matters to concern him. In May, 1853, he was sued by Edward Freeman, a 'frail' blacksmith, for £46-odd, the balance for bolts made for vessels. The jury found for the plaintiff (the paper thought the case too dull to detail!).

The press went into a lot more detail three months later, when Peter was charged with assaulting a John Moor/Moore.

It started over a matter of whether there were herrings to be caught in Scotland!

Peter was heard to tell someone else: "If you believe Jock Moor nobody will believe you."

Moor called Peter "a good-for-nothing fellow" and accused him of treating his (Moor's) wife very badly, and "bringing her to the grave".

Peter allegedly grabbed Moor by the neck and threw him down, then punched him in the face when he got back up.

William Bell, a ship's carpenter, said he'd heard Moor telling Irving not to strike at him, then Irving replying he wanted nothing to do with him. Moor continued talking, and Irving then threw him down. Moor had at some point shaken a spying-glass in Irving's face. Both Bell and a second witness, William Patrickson, had heard Moor say that Irving was the means of driving his wife to an early grave. Patrickson said Moor also called Irving a villain.

The bench decided Peter had been greatly provoked, and dismissed the charge against him.

There's a labourer called John Moore, 58, on the 1851 census in Port Carlisle, with a wife Mary the same age. But no sign of a death for Mary, or any match for 1861 for either.

Silloth versus the west coast

All the while, the Robert Burns was making regular trips to and from Quebec. A sample list of the provisions promised to passengers (it varies a little down the years) was: Adult passengers will each get 2.5lbs of biscuits, 1lb wheat flour, 5lb oatmeal, 2lb rice, 1lb sugar, 2oz tea and 20z salt a week. Yum!

There's also reference to Peter have a brig called the Peace, which carried (for sure) coal.

The Robert Burns was cited in another anonymous letter, signed A Fisherman.This one was again part of the Port Carlisle v Maryport feud, exacerbated by proposals to extend the railway from Port Carlisle to Silloth, and build a four-acre floating dock and harbour there. The idea was to create a port where ships could be loaded/unloaded all year round whatever the state of the tide.

The idea can't have been to Port Carlisle's advantage, either – the canal/railway backers were Carlisle traders who had no special loyalty towards

Port Carlisle. They just wanted the city to have its own port, within easy reach on the Solway. Port Carlisle for them would just be a halt on the way to Silloth, and its railway merely the first stage from Carlisle to Silloth.

That didn't stop them quoting Peter's ship the Robert Burns as an example to criticise Maryport. Specifically John Irving (no relation) of Carlisle referring to the brig having passed over Silloth Bar in April 1854, drawing 14 or 15 feet, while Maryport folk were 'busy clearing mud out of their harbour with barrows and spades'.

Someone signing himself A Fisherman retaliated by saying the ship (having taken on her passengers at Port Carlisle) was brought down the Solway by the Maryport steam tug.

He then gave two more instances of the Robert Burns being taken down by the steam tug, saying on the second, she'd had to be tugged all the way to Maryport. The writer said Peter Irving hadn't ventured into Silloth Bay, and had 'very judiciously declined risking his property' by trying to cross the Silloth bar when the wind blew fresh up the Frith on the second tide, as there might not be enough water over it.

Slates, drains, and Prosperity

In 1854, Peter decided to sell two vessels, both sloops. The Newland is described as being 41 tons register and 60 burthen; the Prosperity as 35 tons

A rough idea of the manorial arms awarded to Peter Irving and his wife Jane, née Simpson

NULLIS CADENTIA VENTIS

register, 55 burthen. Both were said to be in excellent repair, drawing seven feet of water each, when loaded.

However, he seems to have kept the Prosperity, for there are adverts a year later for a cargo of prime herring for sale, on board the Prosperity at Port Carlisle. The advert was running from mid-September to at least October 5, so one can only hope they were preserved in brine, pickled, or smoked!

Later in 1855, he was offering a cargo of Welsh slates for sale off the Prosperity, at Skinburness. They were still being advertised three months later, but then slates don't go off!

There are similar adverts for slates, drains, and herrings, on and off until at least 1867.

Rewind to May 1855 and the saga of the Silloth Bay Railway and Dock Bill.

Peter, described as a merchant and shipowner, was next examined as to the west coast, the nature of the Solway Frith, and the capabilities of Silloth Bay. Peter spoke in favour of Silloth dock, which he thought would be easier of access than Liverpool. And under cross-examination 'remained firm in his statements respecting the deficiencies and inconveniences of the tidal harbours, and the advantages of Silloth Bay'.

Tragedy and too much porridge

The weather struck a blow of its own in February 1856, when a gale destroyed a jetty that was being put up by the promoters of the Silloth Railway and Dock Company. It also caused a sloop belonging to Peter, laden with slates, and 'two flats laden with bricks' to abandon anchorage and 'run away'.

It was a human tragedy that stuck that summer, when three girls drowned in the Solway between Kirkland and Westfield House. Margaret Hinde, 15 and Jane Hodgson, 14, went into the water to bathe. They fell into deep water – the old channel of the Eden – and Isabella Hinde, 13, rushing to help them, met the same fate. Peter was one of several people who ran to try to help, but too late.

He was happy to help on a more joyous occasion that May, officiating when a large model fishing smack was launched at Port Carlisle (before all

involved enjoyed a substantial dinner at The Ship inn). The Carlisle Journal said Peter was "always ready to lend an assisting hand to his neighbours."

He wasn't so keen to help discontented workers. In January 1857, he charged Samuel Craig with running away from the ship Mary, having bound himself to the ship for three years from June 1855. Craig had run away before. The defence said Craig had turned 21 in November and could therefore end his indenture if he wished. Which he did as Peter wouldn't give him any money while he was working on the vessel. Peter wanted to bring some other charge in that case (the report said he was determined to punish Craig), but the court discharged him. There's no sign of him on the 1851 or 1861 census.

It wasn't an apprentice or ship hand but a servant who caused Peter trouble in 1858. A "ruddy-cheeked girl" named Margaret Bendle was charged with leaving the service of her master, Mr. Peter Irving, of Port Carlisle, without cause and before the expiration of her engagement. When charged, she laughed, and the court heard that when Peter had caught up with her and asked her why she'd left, she'd told him: "I don't like the place."

There were roars of laughter in court when she said she'd rather go to jail than back to complete her service – then made it clear it was the food she hadn't liked.

She complained the tea was cold, and she couldn't drink the coffee. Breakfast was poddish, dinner was potatoes and milk, supper was barley meal and havour meal poddish (oatmeal porridge) – but she gave it to the pigs more often than not.

Peter told the court she got the same meals as the family – five meals a day.

The case was dismissed because the court was the wrong place for a breach of service case. Young Margaret 'strutted triumphantly out of court'.

There's a Margaret Bendle aged 13 on the 1851 census at Cardurnock, living with her mother and stepfather. She looks to have been a servant at Barton Vicarage, Westmorland, in 1871 – hopefully, she found the food more to her taste!

A diet of porridge, more porridge, and potatoes and milk for three of the five meals a day doesn't sound very appetising to us today – and young Margaret wasn't the only one who didn't much like it then. For when a apprentice called Cairns jumped ship in Dublin in 1859, just two years into his apprenticeship, the boy's grandfather said he'd been told by one of the crew the boy wanted for victuals.

Peter said the boy had been pretty useless and had cost him £3 in doctor's bills. He was asking for £20 from the grandfather, John Waugh, but agreed to take half plus costs, as it was tough on the old man.

There's a house servant listed with the Irvings on the 1861 census – aged 76!

Sunk by an iceberg

Shipping was a hazardous business to be in, but thus far, Peter (and the crews of his ships) seems to have been lucky, other than the sloop that broke anchorage in 1856. Prior to that, in 1848, the Isabella had gone aground on rocks near Southerness Lighthouse and been wrecked, but the crew and cargo had been saved.

That luck ran out in September 1859, when The Mary grounded on Silloth Bank in a gale and began to fill with water. Her crew of three took to the rigging for an hour or so. The steamer Queen tried a bunch of times, before rescuing them, but a mast then fell

on the Queen, severely injuring ('but not dangerously') the (Queen's) mate, James Buchanan. Mary's mate, Alexander Candlish, was also hurt by the falll of the mast. There was no hope of saving the ship or cargo.

A report of the incident says a lifeboat station should be considered for Silloth. A few months later, Peter was listed among subscribers to Carlisle and Silloth Branch of the RNLI. (The Solway's first lifeboat was launched, with a big ceremony, in June 1860).

Far worse was to follow, with the loss of the Robert Burns, in 1861. There was initially confusion about whether she was crossing from east to west or vice versa, and which port she was heading to/from.

She sank on April 25, but she wasn't reported lost – by Quebec – until May 15, and it took longer for the news to reach home.

Lloyd's List of May 27 reported: 'Quebec – May 15, The Robert Burns (captain Henderson), from Cardiff to this port, is lost in the ice'.

It was reported by other papers early in June that "this fine ship, the property of Mr Peter Irving, of Port Carlisle" had been lost in the Atlantic, "having been run down by an iceberg with several other vessels" on her way home from St John's, Newfoundland.

She is described as having been one of the largest tonnage vessels trading from Cumberland. She was said to have recently left Silloth with a cargo of salt and was to have returned to Port Carlisle laden with timber.

There was 'no intelligence' as to the fate of the crew, and no mention at all of whether she was carrying any passengers. Until, on June 4, the Liverpool Mercury reported that two crew had been rescued from floating ice by the barque Symmetry, and had arrived at Liverpool. The report gives the location of the rescue as latitude 48° 21', longitude 48° 35' – a long way from land.

It was supposed the rest of the crew had perished.

Finally, on June 13, the *Dunfermline Press* was able to tell the story. The Robert Burns had left Cardiff on April 5 with a cargo of coal for the Montreal Ocean Steam Company. The passage had been fine until, at 4am on April 25, she struck a piece of ice on the Banks of Newfoundland, and went down in two minutes, taking the whole crew down to a great depth.

Three of the crew were powerful swimmers and managed to get to the surface and on to the long-boat, which had broken free from the wreck. She drifted alongside the piece of ice and Captain Henderson directed the other two to jump on it. Before he could follow, the long-boat drifted away. The other two – James Irving, boatswain of Annan, and Alfred Read, able-bodied seaman, could see him for six hours, drifting away.

They were luckily picked up by the Symmetry later that day, but despite cruising around all day, there was no sign of the captain or the long-boat.

Some of the crew who perished were subsequently named: Robert Henderson, master, of Annan; William Wilkinson, carpenter, of Harrington; William Smith, cook, of Burgh; Pierre Clouin, a Quebec pilot, sometime resident of Silloth. 'The rest of the crew are strangers'.

Of slates and fish

Peter had been using Messrs. Waller and Graham, of Silloth, as agents to sell slates he shipped to Port Carlisle. But at the end of May 1862, he issued a notice saying they no longer were and all payments should in future be made directly to him. This was to lead to a court case, after a Mr Henderson took some slates to offset a debt he was owed by Waller and Graham. Peter claimed £63 from Henderson, as the slates were his, and the court found in his favour.

There was a bankruptcy hearing for Waller and Graham, timber and slate merchants, Silloth in the summer. The creditors were owed £600 in total – Peter was owed £70. Peter thought £600 was a large sum for the two 'poor men' to have lost in four years, and creditors were asking how it happened. They had well-furnished houses, now empty. He'd supplied slates for them to sell on commission and it seemed they'd used some of the money to buy a very expensive carpet, of which there was now no sign. They seemed to be saying they had lost out on property deals, but had not accounted for all £600.

The case was adjourned, so they could do so.

When the case resumed in September, Waller accused Peter and seven accomplices of breaking into the yard and taking £20 of slates. A lawyer pointed out they were Peter's slates. Both Waller and Graham claimed their furniture belonged to relatives: a mother who lived in Carlisle, and an uncle the lawyer reckoned didn't exist. His Honour suspended the bankrupts' discharge for three months with protection.

There's a Thomas Waller, 30, a carpenter employing six men, living in Caldew Street, Silloth on the 1861 census. There's a Christopher Graham, 32, house joiner next door – which fits a line in the bankruptcy hearings that Graham had been a working joiner before entering into partnership with Waller. And another that they'd lost money on some houses they'd built in Caldew Street.

The recurring subject of fishing rights on the Solway cropped up in May 1864, with a meeting at Carlisle Town Hall over stake-nets illegally placed in the Eden and Esk estuaries. Those present drew up and signed an agreement to jointly take action against those with nets. Peter arrived late and refused to sign it, saying: "I would not take the poor man by the face." (laughter). He probably meant well, but as the Journal pointed out later, stake nets meant a few people got all the fish, leaving nothing for the many and greatly harming the fishery.

Another railway

As I have already covered in the chapter on the Solway Junction Railway, in June 1864, Peter was invited to give evidence to a House of Lords select committee, having petitioned against the viaduct.

It's just worth reminding here that at that point, he was the owner of several vessels, and did a considerable trade shipping coals, slate, manure etc.

Two years later, the House of Commons was told Port Carlisle was barely used as a port now, except by Peter Irving, who lived there and owned vessels.

Peter must surely have been bitterly disappointed – not to mention angry at the inference that his business didn't matter.

The railway was formally completed in June 1868. Peter wasn't to see the first train pass over the viaduct – it didn't open for freight traffic until September 1869. But the works must have affected his business in the final few years of his life.

Back in 1864, it seems he have may have thought 'if you can't beat 'em, join 'em' – an advert for a house to let with 24 acres, mentioned it was only half a mile from the Solway Junction Railway Viaduct, and included the line that it was a most desirable residence for any person connected with the making of the railway. Anyone interested should apply to Peter.

A special presentation

If the address to the House of Lords had been a tough occasion, there was a far pleasanter two months later, when Peter was invited 'by some of the most influential people in the parish of Bowness,' to an evening tea at the King's Arms.

It was a testimonial evening for Peter, who was presented with a silver salver and a gold pen, to acknowledge his service to the parish.

In his acceptance speech, Peter thanked everyone and said there could not be a more gratifying reward than to receive a testimonial of approval and goodwill from so large, influential, and respectable a portion of the parish.

"I beg to assure you that I value in the highest degree the honour which you have conferred upon to-day. which shall handed down to my posterity; and that among all the fortunate circumstances much may have happened to me in the course of my life, I shall feel the event of this day as one of those most deserving of being borne gratefully in mind."

Another loss

Two months after that happy evening, there was another shipping loss that affected Peter. Cumberland barque The Francis Barclay, sailing from Maryport for Dublin, foundered at the entrance of Ramsey Bay. One report says she was likely to become a total wreck. She was owned principally by Peter and insured by Lloyds' and the Maryport Marine Insurance Association.

The barque's usual run appears to have been to and from Quebec. She'd been carrying coals when, one version has it, she struck the Bahama Bank, near the Bahama Light Ship, taking in a lot of water, anchored in the bay and 'drove ashore about two cables length of the North Pier, where she filled with the tide.' The good news was that the crew were all ok, having been saved by a small boat. The barque was just one of many casualties of a gale that had raged for about 17 hours. Four week later, the stern frame with 'Francis Barclay' on it washed up at Port William.

A quieter time

There's not much personal drama on record from then on in Peter's life, though he was a witness in two court cases in 1865.

The first was that of a woman, Mary English, accused of stealing coals from Mrs Thompson and son, of Kirkhouse. Peter had seen her lifting coals from the quay and putting them in a bag. He'd made her put them back and said he'd let her go if she never did it again. He watched the coals for two hours after, during which time she was watching him. He had to go, came back an hour later and the coals had gone. Thomas Robinson of Kirkland House said he saw her and another woman carrying coals, about 100cwt on her back. Mary English denied going back and said they were different coals. She was convicted of larceny, one week's jail with hard labour.

The second was when John Lawson of Campfield was accused of introduction the cattle plague to the area. Peter said he'd seen the cattle pass in front of

his door and they looked as though they'd not eaten in a week; one was 'like a cat on a hot griddle,' hanging its head and slavering. Two other witnesses said they were weak/ill and dull. The bench said it couldn't be proved Lawson knew they had it when he bought them (in Scotland), so fined him £10 rather than £20.

Peter's good service to the parish continued. In June 1866, Wigton Board of Guardians discussed the

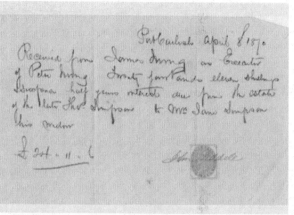

Thomas Simpson was Peter's brother-in-law

chaplain's hours. Peter thought the incumbent's salary should be raised from £15 to £30 – in order that the spiritual wants of the paupers might be better attended to. He certainly thought the chaplain ought to be required to perform his duties to the Union according to the terms of his contract. It was finally agreed that the matter should be brought forward the next meeting of the Board.

Peter attended a number of further Board of Guardian meetings, voting in 1868 for which doctor should carry out vaccinations, and who should be the new clerk. And an 1867 advert tells us he was the honorary secretary of Port Carlisle Baths. The salt baths were to reopen on July 2, in perfect order.

The entry for the plunge baths was 9d; shower baths 6d; hot baths 1s 6d. For three baths or upwards, a reduction of 3d per bath is allowed.

A curious will

Peter Irving died on January 26, 1869, at Port Carlisle. He was 64 and died of pneumonia.

His will has a few of points of interest. For one, he starts by leaving wife Jane her clothes! As well as HIS china, books, prints, glass, etc etc.

Secondly, he makes three sons executors: Thomas, James and PJ. BUT Thomas gets the crumbs.

When wife Jane dies, all children EXCEPT THOMAS are to get £800. Anything left is then to be divided up equally between all the children including Thomas.

Thirdly, he and son James have a bond from the Solway Railway Company. His share of it cost £400.

Lots of lots

In 1891, Peter's executors instructed auctioneers to sell (at the Hope and Anchor): *Lot 1. — 11.854 acres of freehold arable, meadow and pasture land at Glasson, rented by Jacob Whitfield. Lot 2. — A freehold house and garden, at Port Carlisle, rented by Mr R. Harrison. Lot 3.—Two freehold cottages plus a yard, stable and barn, Port Carlisle, rented by F. L. Saul; plus a byre, gig house and calf house in the yard. Lot 4. — Seven freehold cottages and two warehouses adjoining Port Carlisle, in the occupation of Eden Conservancy Board, Mr Richard Poole, Mr John Mackie, and others. Lot 5. — A freehold dwelling house, garden and two cottages, at Port Carlisle, rented by Mrs Selkirk, Mrs Miller, and W. Mark Bell. Lot 6. — Freehold land, a house, outbuildings and garden at Bowness (about 12 acres) rented by Joseph Williamson. Lot 7.—Two freehold cottages and gardens at Bowness, rented by Joseph Boustead and Peter Hunter.*

Peter Irving's will was proved by son James in 1869. James died in 1877. His will was proved by PJ in 1889.

In 1891 (after Peter's widow Jane died), the estate was put up for sale (as itemised above), but no satisfactory offer was made.

PJ bought it himself for £1,800 in April 1896. Having been granted authority in 1895 by the other beneficiaries to buy it at auction for not less than £1,500.

14

The Irving ships

Vessels owned/commanded by members of the Irving family

Ship types

INDIVIDUAL ships were unique – designed for the specific purpose of the owner. But, they all fell within categories, as used in the table above. This book is a general history of Port Carlisle and the Solway coast, and people living there, not a detailed study of any aspect. The following are very basic summaries only.

Schooner
These can have two, three, or four masts, rigged with fore and aft sails. A tonnage list for schooners built at one yard ranges from 50 to 138.

Barque
Beginning of the end of commercial sailing vessels, these had a large carrying capacity – larger than clippers. They mostly had three masts, but could have four or even five. A tonnage list for barques built at one yard ranges from 288 to 357. They could be as much as 300 feet long. The Francis Barclay appears in the 1861 census in Liverpool, listed at home port Port Carlisle, 240 tons, 'foreign trade'.

There is a barque Francis Barclay sailing from the Bird Islands to Liverpool, in 1854, carrying guano. A previous ship of the same name sailed the globe and seems to have been lost in 1853.

Brig
These had two masts, and the tonnage list shows a range from 85 to 338 tons. One source says they

were designed for coastal work and short sea trips. However, the Robert Burns regularly sailed from Port Carlisle to Quebec. Another source says they were most commonly used for carrying cargo over large bodies of water, where following winds could be expected.

The key advantage for Solway owners was that a brig could be easily manoeuvred under sail in restricted spaces and it was well suited for sailings to small harbours where there were no tugs. They could be fast and were about 130 feet in length. The brig was a very old and efficient sailing rig, in use up right to the end of commercial sailing ships.

The brief report of the Robert Burns' sinking describes her as one of the largest-tonnage vessels trading from Cumberland.

Sloop

A fore and aft rigged vessel with a single mast. In the 19th century, most were small inshore fishing vessels. However, in 1834, the sloop Phoebe is recorded as arriving at Port Carlisle with a cargo of iron, from Newport. Assuming there weren't two ships called Prosperity, in 1801 an Irving was her master on a trip carrying wheat, oatmeal, oats, butter, potatoes and bacon.

Smack

A smack is a traditional coastal fishing or merchant vessel, either single- or two-masted. A dictionary defines it as: 'any of various fore-and-aft-rigged fishing vessels of rather large size, often containing a well to keep the catch alive.' The Ann and Mary is listed as a smack in 1840. In 1834, she is listed as an arrival at Liverpool, carrying 'sundries'.

Steamer

Steam ships – or hybrid steam/sailing ships – were already around by the 1830s. However, they were very expensive to build and run, certainly in comparison to sailing ships. Wind may be unreliable, but unlike coal, it is free!

While sailing ships continued to be used for bulk cargoes – such as coal, ironically – steamers were used to carry passengers and mail. In 1854, Peter's sailing brig the Robert Burns was reported to have been towed down the Solway by the Maryport steam tug, another obvious good use for steam power.

The City of Carlisle impressed passengers when she was new in 1814, sailing from Port Carlisle to Liverpool in 12 hours and returning in one tide: a 'tolerably striking proof of the advantages of steam conveyance'.

Sample of shipping intelligence (extracted), May 1837

NB, The names in capitals were the masters that voyage.

***

PORT CARLISLE. — Arrived: City of Carlisle, HUDSON, and Solway, BURTON, (steamers,) from Liverpool with goods and passengers; Thomas, IRVING, in ballast; Newlands, IRVING, in ballast; Prosperity, IRVING, with slates, from Bangor; Phebe, IRVING, with slates, for Duddan;

***

Sailed: City of Carlisle, HUDSON, and Solway, BURTON, (steamers) for Liverpool, with goods and passengers; Ann and Mary, SCOTT, with coals, for Annan; Thomas, IRVING, with British wood, for Water of Urr; Newlands, IRVING, with coals, for Dumfries; Prosperity, IRVING, with coals, for Drogheda; Phebe, IRVING, with coals, for Courtown.

Vessel	Type	Master	Owner	Known date(s)	Lost
Ann and Mary	Smack	Thomas Radcliffe	Peter Irving	1834, 1840	
City of Carlisle	Steamer	James Irving		1834 1840/41	
The Fisher			Peter Irving	1864	
Francis Barclay	Barque		Peter Irving and others		1864
Friends	Schooner		Peter Irving and others	1840	
Isabella	Schooner		Peter Irving and others	1840	1848
Jane	Unknown	James Irving snr	Captain Irving	1803	By 1835
Jane	Brig	James Irving jnr		1834, 1843	
Mary	Schooner	David Irving (1840)	Peter Irving and others	1840	1859
Newland	Sloop		Peter Irving	1837, 1854	
Peace	Brig		Peter Irving	1851	
Phoebe	Sloop	Richard Irving	Margaret Irving & others	1828, 1840	1861
Prosperity	Sloop	Robert Irving	Peter Irving Captain Irving	1837-1855 1801	
Robert Burns	Brig		Peter Irving	1849	1861

NB. I haven't listed known entries where it was just recorded that the master's name was 'Irving', unless there are other references to the same vessel where it is known it was connected to the family. EG. 1810 arrivals/departures include: Prosperity, Irving; Lovely Nelly, Irving; Charles, Irving. I've only added Prosperity, as she for sure was owned by Peter Irving by 1837

15

Peter John Irving

Peter's son was arguably Port Carlisle's biggest hero and adventurer, winning bravery medals, and the Blue Riband – twice

Born about 1848, died 1903, both Port Carlisle

Peter Irving and Jane (Simpson) had four sons and two daughters who survived infancy, but only one, Peter John, was to become a mariner.

Thomas (1832-1888) became a farmer, at Bowness. James (1835-1877) was a sharebroker, who died in Switzerland, with estate 'under £30,000' (he lived in Port Carlisle for a while). Edward (born 1852) also became a sharebroker – after going bankrupt as seed and manure merchant.

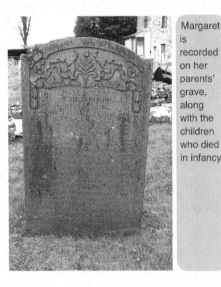

Margaret is recorded on her parents' grave, along with the children who died in infancy

Of the daughters, Rachel (born about 1836) married a master mariner, John Hudson, and moved to Liverpool, then Cheshire.

Poor Margaret (1833-1854) broke her back on October 11, 1853, falling 15 feet from an unlit bridge when alighting from a train at Wreay. The accident left her paralysed 'from high up the back'. She suffered acute pain until her death at home on June 18, 1854.

The mariner of the children was Peter John, who became a captain in the service of the White Star line.

His commands include the RMS Teutonic, and the SS Republic.

An undated description of him refers to him as 'another of the White Star's galaxy of quiet men, and yet he is the sort of officer that always favourably impresses those who meet him' and says he earned his rank on merit.

Bronze medal

In 1875, PJ was awarded a bronze medal for services to shipwrecked seamen of the Oriental, of North Shields.

In January that year, it was reported that the Oriental had been towed into Harwich, much damaged, after colliding with a steamer, which it was feared had foundered. The Oriental was carrying coal and coke for Carthagena when the unknown steamer hit her midships off Newarp Light. The Oriental's bowspit was carried away and she was taking on water. Three tugs, with a lifeboat on hand, brought her into Harwich. The Oriental was a large, full-rigged vessel, upwards of 1,600 tons.

If there is more detail to that story (which steamer? etc), I'm afraid I didn't have the patience to wade through more than 11,000 possible pages to discover.

What is relevant is that the Oriental must have been repaired, as she was back at sea for sure by November.

For on November 18, the crew off the White Star steamer Baltic, spotted signals and changed course.

In terrible seas, they found the Oriental, dismasted and sinking. The remaining 16 crew were burning tar in a barrel on deck, to signal for help. The other ten crew had got off the Oriental in one of her boats the previous day.

All this was learned by the Baltic's captain, Benjamin Gleadell, after Chief Officer Irving had taken charge of her lifeboat. The wreck was rolling and plunging, but PJ and the rescue party got the Oriental's crew safely off in two trips. The wreck caught fire from the tar barrel.

Capt Gleadell kept searching until, the next morning, they found the ten 'deserters,' in a single boat.

The Baltic herself had been damaged by the gale, with five sails torn to ribbons – in fact, had she not been blown off course by it, she'd never have come upon the hapless Oriental. The latter had been sailing from London for St John. The Baltic was heading home from New York.

Passengers from the Baltic signed a letter, praising Capt Gleadell for his humanity and seamanship, and PJ for his skill and judgement.

The Baltic's surgeon said: "Mr. Irving and his crew worked gallantly through the great Atlantic waves, and did so, it need scarcely be observed, at imminent peril to their own lives."

Capt Gleadell died in 1888, of natural causes, in his cabin on the Germanic. By then, he had a number of medals and testimonials of his service in saving lives in various incidents, including a gold watch from the President of the United States.

The Oriental, by the way, was truly an unlucky vessel. She'd lost an ordinary seaman called Cairns overboard nine days before she was wrecked. She sprang a leak in terrible conditions on the 16th and they'd cut the masts off, among other desperate efforts to stay afloat as long as possible.

A Board of Inquiry absolved her captain, Joseph Sanderson, of any blame; but censored boatswain John Brannon and the others who had taken to the lifeboat for 'running away' when the Oriental was sinking, 'thereby cutting off all chance of escape for those left on board'.

A year later, Capt Gleadell and PJ were presented with their Board of Trade bronze medals at a special ceremony in Liverpool. They'd already received a gold medal (the captain) and silver (PJ) from the Humane Society.

Brave rescuers

PJ was in charge of the Republic in February 1883, when it came to the rescue of the steamer Glamorgan, which had hit serious trouble about 450 miles from Queenstown, when caught by a hurricane.

Heavy seas all but wrecked her, carrying away seven men (including the captain) who were on deck at the time. The surviving crew (and passengers) were left desperately bailing and pumping out water from what was left, trying to keep her afloat until such time as another ship came by.

That turned out to be the Republic. In appalling conditions, Peter John Irving launched two lifeboats, which saved three of the Glamorgan's crew – at the cost of one of his own sailor's lives, that of Seaman F Forester. Accounts of how it happened vary, but he and Chief Officer GS Barrett were washed overboard in the rough seas. Barrett grabbed a rope and was rescued, but despite a lengthy search, Forrester could not be found. Both lifeboats were damaged beyond further use in the rescue as well, and conditions were plainly too dangerous to risk more men or boats.

Indeed, the Republic was hardly safe herself, and PJ's priority had to be to try to ensure the safety of his crew and passengers.

Those still on the Glamorgan later said they would have understood if Republic had decided it was simply too dangerous to even stick around, let alone try to assist.

But stick around she did. PJ waited till the gale had dropped enough and the sea had calmed sufficiently to try again, the Republic's boats then safely taking off the remainder of those stranded on the Glamorgan. Another lifeboat was damaged beyond further use, and three men were injured (two seriously), but there was no further loss of life.

In all, some 44 men were rescued, PJ having detained the Republic near the wreck for ten hours in terrible weather to do so.

Medals and thanks

For their gallantry, the New York Life Saving Benevolent Association awarded PJ a gold medal, and the crews of the rescue boats $355. The Humane Society of Boston gave PJ and his first and second officer silver medals, and gave $240 to the crews. The Massachusetts Humane Society gave three silver medals, with bronze ones for the crews, including Seaman Forrester, and $240.

The British Board of Trade awarded a gallantry medal and silver tea/coffee service to PJ, GS Barrett, and second officer WJ Bowman, and bronze medals to the 12 lifeboat crews. Forrester's widow was given £100.

In 1897, PJ had £500 of fire insurance with the Palatine Insurance Co of London and Manchester. He'd written in 'medals' alongside the printed list of items covered.

Compensation culture

While most of those aboard the Glamorgan were eternally grateful for the rescue, an Irish stowaway named Thomas Dowse tried to sue PJ and his first officer, GS Barrett, for $25,000 damages for alleged illegal imprisonment and libel.

The two officers voluntarily attended the British Consulate next time they reached New York, and were taken from there to the sheriff's office and bailed for $5,000 each.

Dowse's case was that when taken onboard the Republic, he had been locked up and accused of being an accomplice to a double murder in Dublin. In fact, he was just an ordinary man who'd stowed away because he couldn't find work in Liverpool and hoped to in New York.

PJ's case was that he had given Dowse a suit of his own clothes and treated him as well as everyone rescued from the Glamorgan. It was only when two of the latter ship's officers had raised concerns about Dowse that he had been detained, until such time as PJ could get legal advice. He'd done so immediately on arrival in New York, and Dowse had then been released.

The New York Tribune probably weren't the only people to think Dowse's legal action a disgrace. No one seems to have found an outcome: was it settled out of court, or laughed out of court? The British press seem to have ignored his 'case' completely.

Censured after a tragedy

The rescue of the Glamorgan's crew and passengers illustrates the responsibilities faced by a ship's captain. As things turned out, PJ's decisions saved them, at the cost of 'just' one of his own men. But the cost could easily have been higher, to the point of the Republic being lost as well. And PJ did have to stop the rescue effort for some hours – knowing what was left of Glamorgan might break up at any time while they watched, helplessly.

Four years later, the consequences of a single wrong decision were illustrated by a tragedy that must have haunted him afterwards. By then, PJ was captain of another White Star steamer, the Celtic (he'd been its second mate in 1874).

On May 19, 1887, the Celtic collided with another White Star steamship, the Britannic, in heavy fog about 350 miles off Sandy Hook, New York. The Britannic was struck amidships by the Celtic, killing at least four of Britannic's steerage passengers.

Celtic's bow was damaged, Britannic's port side was badly damaged and she took on water. But both were able to sail to New York, where an inquiry was

later conducted. Britannic's captain, Hugh Hamilton Perry, was "very severely censured," and PJ was "severely censured." Britannic's second officer, James B Mackenzie, was also censured, for leaving the bridge to the fourth officer in fog, for porting his helm, and for not slowing when he heard the Celtic's whistle.

The short version seems to be that neither captain had slowed their ship as they should given the conditions. Britannic (heading east) was travelling at about 15.5 knots an hour and the Celtic (heading west) at 13.5.

PJ had, when the Britannic's whistle was heard, given the order to slow the engines. Had Britannic done the same, the collision might have been avoided.

Further, while Celtic had been sounding her (fog) whistle as required, Britannic hadn't sounded hers until hearing Celtic's. Nor had Britannic used hers to issue 'change course' messages, as Celtic had. However, by ordering full speed after sighting the Celtic, Captain Perry had probably averted a far more serious disaster.

The inquiry also thought steamship signals were not distinctive enough to send clear messages of intent to other vessels.

First reports of the tragedy had included claims that a panic had ensued and passengers on Britannic had to be threatened with revolvers, and that 12 people had died. 'Mangled bodies' were said to have been 'sewn in sacks and thrown overboard,' with 'tales of gallantry, cowardice and pathos'. Irish paper The Freeman's Journal used every adjective at its disposal to describe the events – and perhaps a very hefty dollop of imagination! The paper's report on how the Celtic's passengers saw things was favourable to PJ: 'alert,' 'vigilant,' 'cool-headed' being its adjectives for him.

The *Eastern Daily Press* thought the real evil was the pressure to complete trans-Atlantic journeys as fast as possible.

The Board of Trade subsequently issued advice, reminding that one short whistle blast mean 'I am going to starboard'. Two was port, three was full speed astern. However, given it says the signals are optional and meant only for cases where the ships can see each other (ie not in thick fog), it doesn't seem much use.

The Board also says it's imprudent to alter course to avoid a vessel you can't see. It also thought changing the rules would add to the dangers of navigation, rather than reduce them.

Both ships were soon being advertised by the White Star Line as 'splendid vessels,' though by January 1888, Britannic had a new captain.

Meanwhile, the pressure on captains to cross the Atlantic at speed continued – and the consequences were lauded by the press.

Two proud records

The Teutonic was launched in 1889. A Captain Davidson was the master in January 1891 and it was some time between then and May of that year that PJ took command.

Celtic's last White Star Line voyage was in February 1891, so assuming he was still her captain, PJ may well have switched to Teutonic after that.

In August 1891, Teutonic took the Blue Riband for the fastest Atlantic crossing. The voyage was from Queenstown, Ireland (today: Cobh), to Sandy Hook.

The Teutonic broke her own record just a few weeks later, sailing in the other direction, with her 'well-known commander Captain Irving' in charge.

The record she set to New York (arriving on August 19) was five days 21 hours 25 minutes, averaging 20.5 knots per hour, the distance 2,788 miles. This was an hour and a half faster than the previous record, set by (fellow Cobh Star Line ship) Majestic just a week earlier.

The record to Queenstown (leaving on September 23) was five days, 16 hours and 31 minutes. The feat had several newspapers describing how 'Captain Irving stood proudly on the bridge' as she arrived in port at Queenstown. The 'able commander' later steamed away for Liverpool.

Among her passengers enjoying the west-bound voyage were Bruce Ismay and his wife Julia Florence.

Whether the poor stokers were as appreciative of the feats is perhaps another matter. The *Clyde Shipping Gazette* reported, after the first success, that the Teutonic's use of forced draught upon an air-tight fire room meant it was not unusual for stokers to pass out from the heat and pressure.

Strychnine is good for you (!)

PJ was involved in a curious case in September 1889 that caused him to write to the home secretary. By then master of the (White Star) liner Germanic, he sent an affidavit at the request of the solicitors of a Mrs Maybrick. It regarded an allegation that PJ had seen the late James Maybrick take arsenic.

PJ said he'd seen Maybrick put the contents of small packet in a glass of water (or wine, in another account) and drink it, but didn't know what it was. It seemed to do him good. PJ added that it was well-known that Maybrick had taken strychnine for years. He agreed with the conviction of Mrs Maybrick, and knew there was something wrong at Battlecrease (Maybrick's home at Aigburth, Liverpool) before it got into the papers.

He'd first met Maybrick in 1878, when he commanded the Republic and Maybrick made the crossing to America to buy cotton.

In the same year, Maybrick's future wife, then about 16 and accompanied by her mother, made the voyage from New York to Liverpool on the Republic.

After their marriage, they'd crossed the Atlantic several times on his ship. PJ described Maybrick as "a mighty good fellow" – but was far less laudatory of Mrs M.

Jim Maybrick, 50, was a well-known Liverpool cotton merchant whose death in May 1889 was thought to be poisoning by strychnine. Mrs Florence Maybrick, who was suspected of murder, was 27. She was ill when arrested. Initial rumours pointed to beef tea – and an unnamed third party.

Florence's mother, Baroness von Roques, begged PJ through the Press for more information that might help her daughter's case – what did he know? What did he mean? Who told him what?

If PJ replied, it wasn't publicly.

The short version of the case is that Florence Maybrick was found guilty of murder, at Liverpool Crown Court, but the death sentence was commuted to life imprisonment.

Maybrick had been addicted to a drug containing arsenic after first taking it in 1874, for malaria. He has in recent years been accused of having been Jack the Ripper.

Familiar names

While in charge of the Republic, Peter John Irving apparently had under him for a while a First Officer called Edward J Smith. Smith seems to have been made captain of Republic in 1887.

And if 'White Star Line' and 'Edward J Smith' (and Bruce Ismay) sound familiar, it's because the company went on to build the RMS Titanic, and Smith was her captain on her tragic maiden voyage. She was travelling at 22.5 knots when the iceberg was spotted. Bruce Ismay was by then the chairman of the White Star Line. He famously (or infamously) survived the sinking.

Family life

PJ didn't live to read about the Titanic disaster: he died at Port Carlisle in 1903, aged 55. He left effects in the UK worth £7,589, and effects in Ireland worth £1,400.

He had married, in Liverpool when he was 27/28. The wedding took place at St Bride's Church on May His wife was Elizabeth McKrune, of 91 Haskisson Street, daughter of James McKrune, gentleman. One of the witnesses was PJ's brother Edward Lawson Irving.

A life at sea didn't make for much of a married life. They were married by licence, rather than banns as presumably he couldn't attend church for the reading of the latter.

The 1881 census has an Elizabeth Irving, 30, master mariner's wife, living with a domestic servant in Brick Road, Wallasey, Cheshire.

There was one child of the marriage: daughter Elizabeth was born in Cheshire in 1895. Her mother died in the same quarter, suggesting it was either in, or as a complication of, childbirth.

PJ shows up on the 1901 census, back on home ground at Bowness. Peter John Irving, 57, retired mariner, born Port Carlisle, with wife Elizabeth, 30, b Dalston, and a servant.

This Elizabeth was his second wife, née Buck, the marriage having taken place in 1897. This marriage produced a son – also Peter John. He was born a few weeks after his father's death, and died aged just 12 and half months old, at the start of December 1904.

Peter John Irving's will

The trustees of the will were two nephews (James' sons): John Bell Irving and Robert James Irving, plus his brother-in-law Alfred Buck, and a solicitor.

Wife Elizabeth, while a widow, gets the furniture, plate, glass etc etc and can live in his house at Port Carlisle. She is also to get £150 (annuity) from the trust created from his real estate in the parish of Bowness. I've explained in the chapter on Peter Irving how PJ bought his father's estate in 1891.

If she remarries/dies, and he has no living children, the trust is to benefit his living kin "EXCEPT the son or grandchildren of my brother Thomas, who shall not take any benefit of this or any preceding trusts."

Whatever Thomas had done to upset their father had also upset PJ, it seems.

PJ's widow had remarried by 1910. Her brother Alfred Buck married PJ's niece Maud Mary Irving.

PJ had shares/bonds in about 20 railway companies, from the Caledonian to the Canadian Pacific to the Colorado and Southern, USA.

He also had shares in the Bank of Liverpool; Eastern Extension, Australasia and China Telegraph Company; the Seacombe and New Brighton Omnibus Company, and; the Liverpool Cold Storage and Ice Company Ltd.

16

Jeffray Peat senior

The Peats were among the first local families who tried to make Port Carlisle prosper. And they played a big part in the 'good years'

Born about 1769, died 1836, Port Carlisle

Details among the stones

Among the family graves that are still about legible at St Michael's, Bowness-on-Solway, is that of Jeffray Peat and his wife Ann (née Lawson). With them are their sons Thomas Lawson Peat, who died in 1802, aged six months, and Joseph,

There are three Peat graves still legible, to varying degrees

who died in 1806 aged one, and; daughters Ann, who died in 1819 aged 12, and Kitty, who died in 1824 aged 10.

Their son John (died 1857) and his wife Elizabeth (died 1881 High Hesket) are also recorded on the same gravestone. But, as I've said in the chapter on them, they are also recorded in Hesket-in-the-Forest, so Elizabeth may have been buried there.

Generations of Peats

Jeffray's grandparents – another Jeff (the grave has him as Jeffry) and Mary are buried close by. Jeffry, who died in 1772, was a yeoman with land at Bowness.

In fact, there were Peats recorded at Bowness in the 1500s, but the line prior to Jeffry is somewhat sketchy.

Jeffry and Mary had nine children, with three dying in infancy. Their fifth child was Margaret, who at 37 was unmarried – and expected to stay that way.

However, in the space of a couple of years, she had an illegitimate son (Jeffray), and married Thomas Dalton, a man 19 years her junior (she outlived him).

Blacksmith, publican, farmer, shipping agent...

When Jeffray married Ann Lawson on February 14, 1793, he was recorded as being a blacksmith. They had ten children, but I've not found any other reference to them beyond the church registers until 1829.

In fact, there are two 1829 references. One is a directory entry, that says Jeffray was running the Hope and Anchor. The second is the death notice for Ann, who died 'at the Binnacle' – ie Port Carlisle.

Things become a little confusing. A local history booklet says: "*Jeffery Peat was the first owner of Habberley Cottage. He lived at the Steam Packet and the Hope and Anchor, and owned land which was sold to the canal company.*

"The Hope and Anchor opened in 1829. The Steam Packet was built in 1780."

An entry outlining why Habberley Cottage and the Hope and Anchor (and 1&2 Greenside) are Grade II listed says: 'Early C19... Habberley Cottage was built first..'

Here's the problem:

1829. November 21. Carlisle Patriot
To let for a term of years (sic), from Candlemas next. That old established public house known by the sign of the Hope and Anchor, situate at Binnacle, in the parish of Bowness, with any quantity of land from 20-80 acres, now in the occupation of Jeffrey Peat.

For the Hope and Anchor to be 'old established' in November 1829 is at odds with the idea it first opened that year. Having said that, it's generally accepted that prior to 1819, there were only two premises in what is now Port Carlisle: Kirkland House and The Binnacle inn.

I suspect (no proof) that Jeffray moved to the Steam Packet late in 1829 because his wife had just died (in September). That was also the year his son John had married and it looks as though John and his young family moved to the Steam Packet between 1831-33. It would have been a lot for one man to run, and he may have wanted to ensure his son had a good future.

Given that his son Jeff is shown on an 1836 canal company plan as being – well, it looks like it's either Greenside or Habberley – I wonder if Jeff senior set him up there.

By the time an 1834 directory was published, Jeffray was for sure at the Steam Packet. He was also an agent for a ship owner. There are several adverts in 1833 for a barque called the Lancaster, and a copper-fastened sailing ship called the Balfour, sailing from respectively Annan and Whitehaven, to Quebec. Would-be passengers were invited to apply to one of several people, including Jeffry Peat, Bowness. Unlikely to be Jeffray junior, who was just a labourer.

...and fisherman

The Solway has for centuries been synonymous with salmon. It is also famous for its haaf nets, as covered in the chapter on fishing.

These days, it is strictly regulated, with licences limited, to protect fish stocks.

In bygone days, there was also a close season for salmon. And there were major disputes over who had the right to fish where.

In November 1832, a man called David James was charged with taking salmon during the prohibited period of September 15 to March 10.

James' defence was that he'd used a winter net that only caught flounders. If he were convicted, it would put a lot of poor families out of work and stop the supply of flounders to the Carlisle market.

Jeffray Peat, of the Binnacle, was sworn as a witness. He told the court he had great experience as a fisherman and always used nets such as that produced.

When cross-examined, he denied that the net could hold a salmon. But when pressed, he acknowledged "it would never do to swear against themselves" (the fishermen).

James and two others convicted, but gave notice of appeal.

Jeffray Peat died on Christmas Eve 1836. But he was remembered long after – as a fisherman.

In 1859, there was a lengthy case about salmon fishing – at its heart, the Earl of Lonsdale claiming that he owned all the foreshore covered at high water by the sea and no one else had any right to set nets there.

The defendant was man named Joseph Fell, who claimed he had a right to fish there that was sanctioned by custom immemorial. The jury were told the defence had to prove this custom had existed since the time of Richard I.

Witness John Thompson was 82, so had been born about 1777 – about seven years after Jeffray.

He told the hearing: "I remember a raised net used by Jeffray Peat and Peter Brough. I helped Jeffray Peat to fish with a trap for ten years. The net was more than 100 yards long. The stakes stood 6 or 7 feet above the ground…

"The landowners claimed rent from Peat and Brough, but they would not pay.

"Brough had a property in the town. Peat occupied a house."

Another witness, Robert Brough, who was 83, said around 63 years earlier, the landowners had put up

Hard to read now, even up close

a net at Bowness, which they had sold to his father and Jeffray Peat when they had tired of it. His father and Jeffray had used it for several years, repairing it at the end of each season.

Pattinson Lawson (1787-1865), of Bowness Hall, said he'd been collecting fishing rents for Lord Lonsdale since 1843 (*see chapter on PL*). There had been a trap net yearly opposite Port Carlisle put up by the landowners around 1803/04. Lord Lonsdale's then agent had demanded rent for it, which wasn't paid, so it was taken out.

After three days of all this, the jury found in favour of the Earl, who was awarded damages of (just) one shilling!

One line in the case, from John Topping ('nearly 60 years'), says: "Peat lived nearly all his time at Bowness and Port Carlisle."

If only he'd elaborated a little!

Executors, but no will

In 1877, it was reported that there had been sold, at auction, a double dwelling house, cottage, and garden, situate at Port Carlisle, and owned by the executors of the late Mr Jeffery Peat.

Does 'double dwelling house' suggest Greenside?

Sadly, there is no will to be found in Carlisle Archives to tell us who were his executors, or give us a clue (from the conditions of the will) why they were selling a house 40 years after Jeffray's death.

Dramatis personae

Of the other people mentioned in court cases above...

David James

The man convicted of catching salmon in the close season, in 1832.

The 1841 census has labourer called David James, aged 50, living at Glasson. He is followed by Deborah, 50; Rodger, 20; Richard, 20; Mary, 15; Esther, 14; David, 11, and; Elizabeth, 4.

Joseph Fell

Sadly, (on the 1851 census) there are half a dozen Joseph Fells who could have gone on to be the defendant in the 1859 case. Meanwhile, in contrast, there is no sign of a John Thompson with any Solway connection.

Robert Brough

One of the witnesses in the 1859 case.

He shows up on the 1841 census at Bowness, as a farmer. He's 63, and with him are Margaret, 55; stone masons Peter, 25 (*see the fishing chapter*), and Robert, 19; ag lab John, 17; Abigail 20, and Jane, 5. Ten years later, he is widowed, son John is with him, and so are daughter Abigail. She is now married to a Robert Holmes, with three small children.

Robert is still with Abi and family in 1861 – now described as a fisherman, as is his son-in-law.

Pattinson Lawson

Is worthy of his own chapter.

17

Jeffray Peat junior

Trying to make sense of a
gravestone that didn't add up
led to a curious story

Born about 1797, drowned 1844 in the Solway

"And they all lived happily ever after." We are all
brought up hearing fairytales that end in a wedding
and the assurance that the hero's and heroine's
troubles are over.

But in the real world, marriage isn't always 'till death
do us part'. And while most of our ancestors stayed
together 'for better, for worse,' that was often only a
reflection of the fact that until recent times, divorce
simply wasn't an option.

On the other hand, the 'shame' of illegitimacy we
imagine they held wasn't always the case, either.
Indeed, a look at many marriage certificates and
first-born birth certificates show that even in the
supposedly prim Victorian era, many a blushing
bride had a bump under her wedding dress.

Not all pregnancies led to marriage.

In 1868, the rate of illegitimate births per 1,000 live
births is shown as 58 for England and Wales overall.

The figure was 107 in Cumberland and 100 in
Westmorland.

The Journal of the Statistical Society of London
noted if you drew a line from Suffolk to the Bristol
Channel, every county below would show a
below-average rate, with theories on the subject
wide and varied.

To recap a little on the family background, when
spinster Margaret Peat married Thomas Dalton, at
St Michael's, Bowness-on-Solway, in 1772, the
register notes she was 42 and he was 23.

She'd already surprised folk by having an illegitimate
son, Jeffray (senior), when she was about 38.

He in turn married local woman Ann Lawson on a romantic date: Valentine's Day, 1793. Less romantic is their daughter Mary's baptism date: 17 November 1792.

Always do the maths!

Jeffray and Ann had a son Jeffray, who was born about 1796 and drowned in the Solway on September 28, 1844.

The gravestone in St Michael's churchyard records his first wife, Margaret, as having died on June 22, 1837.

It also lists as 'their children' two infant deaths – with dates that show both were born after Margaret had died!

In fact, the children's birth certificates show their mother was Mary née Blenkinsop, with first daughter Ann born July 29, 1838.

It gets 'worse': when Jeffray married Mary, in March 1838, she is described as a minor. Even if, as census entries suggest, she was born in 1821, she was 17 and heavily pregnant by a man of 40/41, who had got her pregnant around four months after his first wife died.

Perhaps it was embarrassment that led to the 'lies' on the gravestone: Mary (who is also on there, with her second husband, Joseph Thompson) letting the world believe two of her children were those of another woman.

Apart from his voting preferences (Aglionby and Graham), the earliest references I found to Jeffray junior was in 1833, when a grand jury decided to ignore bills by a Robert Bone and Richard Cowen for assault against JJ, and against JJ for an assault on

Bone and Cowen. There's a Bone and a Cowen in Cargo, Stanwix, in 1841, but without more detail…

JJ is described in some sources as a mariner, in others as a labourer, and always of Port Carlisle.

An 1836 plan for the proposed new dock shows 'Jeffery Peat junior' as being – well, it's either Habberley Cottage or Greenside.

However, the 1839 tithe map shows Jeff (his father had died by then) as being at the Hope and Anchor.

When Mary registered their son Jeffery's birth in 1843, she told the registrar JJ was a yeoman.

He told an inquest in 1839 he was a labourer. The dead man was Joseph Shackley, master of a lighter called Despatch, which belonged to the Carlisle, Annan and Liverpool Steam Navigation Company and plied its trade between Carlisle and Annan.

The Despatch

JJ told the inquest he'd been on board the Despatch, which was coming up the Solway between 9pm and 10pm, towing the canal company's Clarence steam boat.

A schooner called Hope, going down the Solway, had struck Despatch, causing the latter's mizen mast to collapse. It landed on Captain Shackley, at the helm. He died of the resulting injuries

Joseph Shackley left a widow and large family 'entirely unprovided for'.

The 1841 census shows JJ living in Port Carlisle with Mary and their baby daughter Elizabeth, aged two weeks. JJ is listed as 43, Mary as 20. Also with them is Elizabeth Topping, 15 – daughter of JJ's sister Margaret (Peat) and Robert Topping.

The next inquest in which JJ features was his own. He and Jonathan Sharp, of Glasson, were labourers working for the Carlisle, Annan and Liverpool Steam Navigation Company.

That night in 1844, a ship called the Victoria was heading for Annan to take on cargo for Liverpool. Victoria was towing a lighter, and the lighter was in turn towing a sailing boat, the Emerald.

JJ and Sharp were on board the Emerald – which began to sink soon after the three vessels cleared the Port Carlisle jetties.

JJ was seen clinging to the masts, until the boat disappeared. Sharp wasn't seen. Two boats were lowered to try to rescue them, but it was too late, and their bodies were washed up near Bowness the following morning.

Jonathan Sharp left a wife and six children penniless. the 1814 census lists him as a joiner, aged 45, followed by Jane, 35; Elizabeth, 10; Esther, 8; Isabella, 5; John, 3; Mary, 1, and: Elizabeth Sanderson, 3 months (she looks to have been the illegitimate daughter of a Mary Sanderson).

As for JJ's young wife...

Her marriage certificate (to JJ) says she's a minor, a spinster, a servant, living in Port Carlisle. Under 'father,' it says Thomas – looks like Watman, yeoman. Certainly nothing like Blenkinsop.

When she registered the birth of son Jeffrey, her maiden name was given as Blenkinship.

The only 'candidate' I've found, births-wise, is a Mary Blenkinship born to a Betty, single-woman, and baptised in Holme Cultram in 1822. That fits her father having a different surname.

I hope that is the wrong Mary. Because if she was baptised at a few weeks, or even a few months, it means she was 15 when she married, and still 14 when JJ got her pregnant. He was, as mentioned before, 40/41.

An 1844 'to let notice' describes 'a commodious dwelling house at Port Carlisle, comprising eight rooms with attics above, a scullery and an excellent cellar. For particulars, please apply to Mrs Mary Peat.'

Mary remarried, in May 1846. Her second husband, Joseph Thompson, was ten years older than her and a Bowness mariner. They had seven daughters (one dying in infancy). She, Joseph, and daughters Margaret and Judith are named on the gravestone of JJ and Margaret, and the two children Mary couldn't (or didn't) publicly acknowledge were actually hers.

18

Elizabeth Simpson

Elizabeth was the sister-in-law of Peter Irving and daughter-in-law of Jeffray Peat senior. She was also a strong woman with a kind smile

Baptised 1802, died 1881 High Hesket

It may seem strange to have 'favourites' on a family tree who died so long ago you can have little idea what they were like as a person.

But sometimes what facts you can glean warm you towards some of them. And that's the case with Elizabeth Simpson.

Elizabeth was baptised at Aikton (her birthplace is also given as Quarrygill, on censuses). She was the third of six children of Thomas Simpson (circa 1772-1845) and Rachel Willan (circa 1774-1855), whose grave can be found in the churchyard at Bowness.

Thomas had married Rachel in 1798 in Thursby, but it looks as though they'd settled at Bowness by 1818, when a Thomas Simpson bought a share in the proposed Carlisle Canal. For sure, they were there by 1833, according to polling records.

Thomas was a yeoman farmer. His and Rachel's fourth child, Jane, was to marry Peter Irving in 1831. Eldest daughter Mary had married a Bowness farmer, John Lawson, in 1820. The other children were sons: John, Thomas and Edward.

Family life

Elizabeth married at Bowness on March 28, 1829. Her husband was John Peat (1795-1857).

117

John was variously (and simultaneously) a publican, farmer, land owner and gig proprietor, who died in 1857, aged 62 – of an enlarged liver. It's hard not to speculate that perhaps he was a little too jovial a host!

Elizabeth had by then borne 13 children, and buried four. She was 29 when she had the first (rather soon after marriage!) and around 49 when she had the last.

Following the old custom of 'reusing' names after a child died, there were to be three Rachels and three Johns. The last John (1851-1878) is noted on the 1871 census (only) as being an 'imbecile'. Could this have been Down's? He was left rents and then properties in his uncle John Lawson's will, written in 1858, with reference to his education, so presumably aged seven, his family didn't consider him to be 'an imbecile'.

The Steam Packet

I was told by my great aunts that John Peat was a sea captain, who owned what is now Hesket House (then the Steam Packet Hotel) in Port Carlisle, and that he built/had built the neighbouring row of cottages for his children.

He was certainly at the Steam Packet, but I can find no record of his having been at sea before that. Although he didn't marry until he was 34, and there's no record of him having done anything else before marriage, either.

There is a newspaper report in 1822 of a court case involving several men accused of looting a wreck (the Grampus). A John Peat, fisherman at Skinburness, gave evidence as a witness for the prosecution, saying one of the men in the dock had told him he had articles from the wreck. However, there were other John Peats of an age to be the

fisherman. The part about the cottages is backed up, both by a local history leaflet and by his will: they were farm outbuildings and John had them converted for his six daughters.

A publican and land owner

Life for John and Elizabeth doesn't seem to have thrown up any great dramas, beyond the grief of losing two children as babies and two as infants.

John was described as a husbandman of Bowness at the baptism of their first daughter, Rachel, in 1829. She died in 1830.

Their second, also Rachel, was five. The family were 'of Bowness' when she was baptised in 1831; she died in 1836, 'at the Binnacle.'

This may mean the old Binnacle pub. More likely, it was just another way of saying 'Port Carlisle'.

They were 'of Fishers Cross' in 1833 – with John described as a carrier. And he had the same occupation in 1835, when they were recorded as being 'of Fishers Cross/Binnacle'.

Given that John's father Jeffray was at the Steam Packet in 1834 (he died in 1836), I suspect it was a case that they were living together at that stage, and John took over the licence when his father died.

In 1841, John was described as a publican, and as well as five children, the household included five young servants. In 1851, it is recorded that as well as being a publican, he was also farming 50 acres. The 1839 tithe map shows some of this land was long, narrow strips alongside the canal.

In 1847, he was listed in a directory as an innkeeper, and horse and gig proprietor, at the Steam Packet, and a carrier to Wigton three times a week. He is also mentioned as an overseer of the poor (1850) and surveyor of the local roads/sea wall (1857)

When John died, in 1857, he left the bulk of his estate to Elizabeth, for herself and the children while they were under age. Eldest son Jeffery would inherit it all when Elizabeth died.

Sons Thomas and John were bequeathed plots of land bought off the Carlisle Canal Company. And daughters Rachel, Ann, Elizabeth, Mary, Jane and Catherine were each to get one of the cottages, with Mary and Jane also bequeathed adjacent shops.

Via The Ship to Kirkland House

Elizabeth was left a widow, in her mid-fifties, with Elizabeth (20), Mary (17), Jane (not quite 13), Catherine (10), and John (7) very much dependent on her. Older daughters Ann and Rachel were 22, and still single. And sons Jeffery (25) and Thomas (23) were also still at home.

So, what did Elizabeth do?

She knuckled down and carried on – aided by her older children.

An 1858 directory lists her at the Steam Packet. That year, there was auctioned at Glasson a 'good and substantial farmhouse,' outbuildings and more than 32 acres of farmland 'in the occupation of Mrs Peat, Thomas Lawson and the late John Ridley'.

Christmas that year saw some of the local folk enjoying themselves! For the following month, three women innkeepers faces prosecution for selling drink on Christmas Day, when the pubs should have been shut. The other two cases couldn't be made to stick, but Mrs Peat, 'landlady of The Ship,' was fined 10 shillings plus costs.

More auctions followed. In March 1861, at Port Carlisle, she sold 14 head of cattle, three horses, six pigs, seven stacks of grain, one stack of hay, ten tons potatoes, and turnips etc. In February 1862, there was a 'to let' notice for 25 acres of arable and meadow land adjoining what was now the railway (rather than the canal), along with a cottage and garden, at Glasson Creek Bridge, 'lately in the occupation of Mrs Peat'.

She may well have relied on her sons Jeffery and Thomas to do the 'heavy lifting,' but she was still in charge. When the cattle plague hit Cumberland in 1866, it's her name on a list of farmers affected. One update, on April 6, says there had been 454 new cases since the previous week, affecting 30 more farms. Elizabeth was lucky in that none of her cows had died of the plague and just one had had to be destroyed. The cottages and shops John Peat had created for his daughters, meanwhile, were still bringing in rent for the family.

By 1871, she'd given up the pub trade, but not to take life easy. For at some point between 1867 and then, the family had taken over Kirkland House. The census lists her as farming 120 acres.

It also lists her as being 60! It's tempting to think she knocked a decade off her age, rather than the enumerator making the error.

She would actually have been around 69 (I haven't got her birth date, only the baptism). And she was still involved in the family business, selling butter every Saturday in Carlisle Butter Market.

The Peats were only at Kirkland House for a few years. By 1878, Jeffery had taken over the White Ox, at High Hesket. He had taken on responsibility for the family, as not only did Elizabeth go there with him, but also his brother Thomas, his sister Mary, her son Edward, his sister Ann's son Thomas, and his brother John.

Not that Elizabeth put her feet up. On June 12, 1878, members of the Court Loyal Tarnwadling no 757 of the Ancient Order of Foresters held their 30th anniversary and procession, starting in Armathwaite. As well as parades round and between villages, with a brass band, and a church service, the lodge members enjoyed 'an excellent dinner provided by Mrs Peat' in the lodge room of the White Ox.

Elizabeth died on January 10, 1881, aged 79. Her name is listed on gravestones at both Bowness (where he was for sure buried) and at Hesket-in-the-Forest.

A fitting occasion

Her life may not seem the most interesting, or dramatic in this book. But she has always struck me as resilient.

And on her photo, she has a kind smile.

She'd not become a mother until she was 29, but had 'made up for lost time' by then being repeatedly pregnant over the course of the next two decades, including a set of twins. She'd had to bear the loss of two babies, two infant children, and two adult children (daughter

Elizabeth died at or soon after childbirth, in 1869; son John died, aged 27, in 1878). She'd had to cope with widowhood while still responsible for her children and rather than rely on the income she inherited (from the cottage rents, and from a legacy from her father), she carried on working, and saw to it that the whole family could stay together – including daughter Mary's illegitimate son Edward.

I am writing this chapter on Mother's Day. Elizabeth (Simpson) Peat seems a good person to be writing about today.

An old photo of the Steam Packet (Hesket House), from the family album

19

The Peat twins

Ann Peat, born 1836, died 1902

Rachel Peat, b 1836, died 1894

"I'm 'enery the Eighth, I am... I got married to the widow next door, she'd been married seven times before. Every one was an 'enery..."

For the Peat twins of Port Carlisle, it wasn't eight Henrys. But, they did manage six husbands between them; and five of them were called Thomas.

Their story illustrates what life could be like for women in the 19th century.

A curious pattern

Ann and Rachel Peat were born in 1836, the fifth and sixth children of John and Elizabeth Peat. Rachel was the third daughter to be named after Elizabeth's mother (the previous two having died). Ann was named after John's mother. Rachel is described as 'second surviving daughter' in one record, so she was the younger twin.

It is purely coincidence, but for the twins, life was to follow a curious pattern, for both were to marry three times.

- Their first marriages were both in 1860.

- Their second marriages were both in 1876.

Sadly, I'm not sure which twin is which

- Their first husbands were both about a year older than them.

- Their second husbands were both much older than them – 26 years and 33 years.

- Their third husbands were both ten years older than them.

- And apart from one John, the husbands were all called Thomas.

No quiet backwater

Today's visitors to Port Carlisle may think of it as a sleepy spot, miles from the nearest 'hub' of urbanisation.

But while Port Carlisle was already 'tailing off' in as a port by the 1850s, the Peat family's home, the Steam Packet, would still have been a busy hotel, providing accommodation for those passing through at the start or end of voyages.

It is little surprise, then, that Ann's first husband, Thomas Bell, was a sea captain from Liverpool. Nor was it difficult for her to travel there to get married, which she did (by licence) on September 18, 1860. The marriage certificate simply says 'mariner,' but a newspaper notice says he was then Chief Officer of the (clipper) Pizarro.

Rachel's first husband, John Matthews, was a tailor who'd been apprenticed locally and was a Cumbrian.

They married at Bowness on April 30, 1860, and the certificate gives his address as Kirkbride, though the newspaper notice says he was 'of London'.

The first husbands

Ann stayed at home with mum while Captain Bell was at sea. He was away for the 1861 census, but did register the birth of their first child, John, at the end of July – he gives his rank as 'mate in the

This is either Rachel and John, or Ann and Tom

merchant service'. By the time son Thomas came along, in 1864, Tom was a master mariner (ie, a captain). Two more children followed: William Jeffery in 1866, and Mary Ann (Polly), in 1869. Ann and the children were at Kirkland House with her mother on the 1871 census, with Ann described as a captain's wife.

Tragedies and misery

But, some time between then and 1876, Tom was 'lost at sea'.

Sadly, my great-aunts (source of family knowledge!) knew no more than that, and I have been unable to trace him or what happened. The Pizarro went missing crossing the Atlantic in the winter of 1872, but her captain on that fateful voyage was a G Matthews.

Whenever and wherever poor Tom died, Ann was left a widow with four dependent children.

Meanwhile, Rachel and John had moved after their marriage to the East End of London, initially to a lodgings house in Heath Street, Mile End Old Town (Tower Hamlets/Stepney).

The contrast for a woman brought up on the shores of the Solway, must have been terrible.

And Rachel's marriage vows – 'for better for worse, in sickness and in health' – were sadly to be very much tested.

They had to watch their son John suffer for more than three months with acute hydrocephalus (fluid on the brain), with no hope of a cure, before dying aged two, in January 1864, still in the lodgings house at Heath Street.

They went on to have two daughters: Mary Lawson Matthews was baptised in Stepney in January 1865; Elizabeth Ann was born on February 1, three years later.

The sisters were buried together, in Tower Hamlets Cemetery, on April 13, 1872.

Mary's death certificate shows she'd had 'pertiasis' for 21 days, and broncho pneumonia for seven. I haven't got her sister's certificate.

The family were then living in Diggon Street. Booth's Poverty Map shows this as 'Fairly comfortable. Good ordinary earnings', but that was no protection from the diseases of urban life.

Having buried three children, John's days were also numbered. He had contracted phthisis (consumption – TB) late in 1871 – and Rachel had 18 months of seeing him ill and finally dying, in Diggon Street, in June 1873.

Love or practicality?

So by 1873, Rachel was widowed, far from all her family and had lost her children. Ann was widowed with four children. What were their options? They could open their own lodging house, they could take in washing. Or, they could find husbands.

Which is what both did.

On June 26, 1876, in Bakewell, Derbyshire, Rachel married a widower called Thomas Scott. She was 40, he was 66.

The census returns show him as having been born at Greystoke. In 1876, he was a land agent, living in the Derbyshire hamlet of Matlock Bank.

What took Rachel to Derbyshire can only be guessed at, but leaving London far behind her is very understandable – even if doing so meant leaving John and their three children behind, in Tower Hamlets Cemetery.

On June 4, 1876, Ann married Thomas Knox, a gamekeeper of Low Hesket, Cumberland, who was born on the Isle of Man but had lived in Cumberland since at least 1830, the date of his first marriage. He shows up on the 1841/51/61/71 censuses as living at Barrock Lodge/Barrock Park Cottage. On the marriage certificate, Ann's address is given as High Hesket – her brother and mother were running the White Ox there by 1878 for sure.

When Thomas Knox married Ann, she was 40, he was 75. His children by his first wife were older than Ann.

Alone again

The second marriages didn't buy the twins security for long. Thomas Knox died in 1881. Thomas Scott died in 1883.

Ann's children, by the way, had been scattered by her circumstances. On the 1881 census, only William (who was 14) was with her in Low Hesket. John was 19 and making a life for himself; Thomas was at the White Ox, with the 'bulk' of the Peat family; Polly, aged 12, was with (her aunt) Rachel and (uncle) Thomas Scott, in Graham Street, Penrith.

Although both Thomas Knox and Thomas Scott left their wives a decent legacy, they were now widows again, and still only in their 40s.

So, on September 28, 1882, Ann married Thomas Walker, of High Hesket, a grocer. She was 46, he 56.

And on December 17, 1888, Rachel married 'landed proprietor' Thomas Winskell, in Carlisle. She was 52, he was 63.

In 1878 a Thos Winskell of Fern Bank, Penrith, had witnessed the will of Thomas Scott, Rachel's husband. Can't be a coincidence.

The legacies

Rachel died in December 1894, in Penrith, leaving effects worth £131 (worth the equivalent of around £11,000-13,000 today). She named her sister Kate Leslie as the executrix, and left a gold watch and chain to her niece Lilly Leslie.

She left her furniture, clothes, and other articles of household and personal use to sister Kate.

The rest went to sisters Annie Walker and Kate Leslie in equal shares.

The will was witnessed by Mary Ann Bell, High Hesket (ie her niece) and Sarah Cumberland, Carlisle.

Thomas outlived her by just five months.

Ann died in July 1902, outliving two of her four children and leaving Thomas Walker effects worth £186 13s.

When he died in 1914, he named Ann's son John Bell as one of the executors (his own nephew Ralph Nixon was the other). Her granddaughter Annie Jane Bell got £20, John got £5 for his trouble. And after other bequests, the rest of the estate was divided equally between Ralph, John Bell, and John's brother Thomas.

Given he had a wealth of nephews and nieces of his own to choose from, it surely says something that Thomas made Ann's sons two of the three main beneficiaries.

A dramatic footnote

This being a book about Port Carlisle, the following isn't strictly relevant. But it's so dramatic it seems remiss not to briefly mention it.

Annie Jane Bell's (single) mother Polly died either having her or very soon after, in 1901. Annie Jane was adopted by a Joseph Nixon (no obvious relation to Ralph) and his wife Mary Ann, who lived at Lance Moor, Newby, in Westmorland.

They were murdered in 1933 – shot dead by a neighbour called Richard Hetherington, who then burned down their isolated bungalow, trying to cover his crime. After a jury convicted him, Hetherington was hanged at Walton prison, on June 20, 1933, still denying his guilt.

20

Pattinson Lawson

Not a Port Carlisle man, but worth stretching things to include him!

Baptised 1786, Bowness-on-Solway, died June 1865, Bowness Hall

Although this book is primarily about Port Carlisle, it would be a shame to leave out Pattinson Lawson just because he lived a short walk away. Especially as my notes for him are headed:

Eloped with one wife, guilty of assault, riot victim.

And he features in fishing matters, as from 1843, he collected fishing rents for Lord Lonsdale – when he could get people to pay them, that is! Although not everyone believed he was entitled to collect them.

Family background

Brothers John and Pattinson Lawson (hereafter PL) were both baptised on June 26, 1786. Their parents were John Lawson and Mary (Pattinson). PL was to tell a court decades later that he had come to Bowness around 1800 – the baptism at St Michael's suggests the move was a local one. The 1871 census says he was born at Whitrigg.

John senior died at Bowness Hall in 1831, leaving a very long and complex will. The fact his housekeeper, Nancy Carruthers, was left £200 is perhaps enough to show he was wealthy.

Pattinson Lawson is actually named on two memorial stones at St Michael's

John senior and Mary are buried at St Michael's, and are named on the same grave as Pattinson Lawson:

Mary Lawson of Bowness Hall d Feb 26, 1816, aged 72. John d 21 Dec 1831, aged 89.

It then drops down to a new panel, and names PL's first two wives.

PL married Ann Ritson (1786-1820), of Maryport, in 1815, at Crosscanonby. He married Rhoda Askew (1797-1825) in November 1821, at Bowness. And finally, he married Mary Collinson (1804-1888), in June 1834, also at Bowness.

1816 – The Year without a Summer

There were food shortages in many countries in the early years of the 19th century. The Napoleonic wars had already taken a toll on Europe, and there were a series of volcanic eruptions, from 1809-14. They had already chucked up a lot of dust into the atmosphere, when in 1815, Mount Tambora (on the island of Sumbawa, Indonesia) erupted big-time. The dust in the atmosphere blocked sunlight from reaching the Earth – it created a 'nuclear winter' effect that hit agriculture.

Around the world, crops failed, prices for those that didn't rose. There were major food shortages, leading to famine. And in some places, desperate people turned to desperate measures.

The Allonby riots

On March 4, 1817, a 'great number of the lower classes' broke into a storehouse in Allonby, stealing flour, oatmeal and pearl barley, belonging to corn and meal merchant Pattinson Lawson. It was to have been shipped to Liverpool on a vessel then lying in Allonby Bay.

The following day, they returned, in greater numbers – one report puts it as 600-700 – and took what they'd not been able to carry the first time. It amounted to about 20 tons in all.

Some of the mob also went to a mill, but on being told by the owner that its contents belonged entirely to him and his neighbours, they left.

It would seem there was a certain 'Robin Hood' sentiment of 'justified' theft: stealing grain that was to be shipped to Liverpool was justifiable, stealing food from the mouths of locals was not.

Indeed, the *Carlisle Patriot* reported that the thieves called the grain "our own".

The cavalry were called out from Carlisle, and special constables were appointed to quell the troubles. Damage was put at 'not exceeding £300'. "Which sum Mr Lawson will endeavour to recover by legal proceedings from the hundreds of rioters."

A lot of the stuff was wasted, strewn along the roads as the rioters fled with it. And it was suggested that not all of them had been motivated by want – as with any riot (to this day), there were those who just jumped at the chance to cause damage and to steal, purely because there is 'safety' doing so as part of a mob.

There were 92 arrests, but no one in Maryport or anywhere else was telling tales on the ringleaders – one can't imagine PL recovered much by way of compensation.

'You pay': 'No, you'

PL did, however, seek recompense from the owner of the warehouse, fish curer Joseph Sim. After the first attack, Mr Sim and his neighbours had moved nine sacks of oatmeal to a byre, to safeguard it. Later, it was moved to Mr Sim's parlour, for greater safety.

PL summoned Mr Sims before Maryport magistrates for the return of the meal. Mr Sim's response was that first, PL had to pay for moving and looking after the meal, and for damage to his warehouse – about £20. PL offered him £3, which Sim refused.

The oatmeal then became damp and 'so offensive' it had to be thrown on the dunghill.

In August 1819, Mr Justice Bayley advised a jury that while Sim could have fairly charged PL for looking after the meal, and his trouble saving it, no way could he charge PL for the warehouse damage. And given that the meal had been spoiled, it was clearly down to Sim to make good.

The jury found for PL and awarded him £20 damages.

The riot wasn't the only crime he suffered. In 1821, a 22-year-old labourer called Joseph Street was sentenced to seven years' transportation for stealing poultry, potatoes etc from him.

PL for sure could have done with some money, for in 1822, he went bankrupt, with the dividend date announced two years later.

Who was where, when

PL's father John, as I've said, left a complex will.

As I read it, John left Bowness Hall his to his nephew Richard, a customs officer of Drumburgh.

John's son Richard got other land and property (a windmill, corn mill, and kiln) at Bowness. And PL got land and property elsewhere at Bowness.

However, nephew Richard stayed put at Drumburgh. And PL stayed at Bowness Hall after his father died.

Flying on the wings of love

As I've mentioned above, PL married three times. His first wife, Ann Ritson died at Bowness Hall on October 10, 1820, aged 34.

PL and Ann had two daughters: Betsy died in March 1822, aged three; Mary Ann died in 1841, aged 24.

PL's second wife, Rhoda (daughter of Joseph Askew and Ann née Heskett) died in October 1825, less than four years after they married. She was 28 and there are no named children.

It was PL's third marriage that caused something of a stir. The *Whitehaven Herald* claimed: '*a Cupid-stricken couple, flying on the wings of love, decamped from Keswick on Saturday last, amid the pelting of the pitiless storm, it is supposed for Gretna.*'

The couple were Mary Collinson, only daughter of the Reverend Thomas Collinson, of Threlkeld, near Keswick: her 'lord elect' was PL of Bowness Hall. Mary was 30, and PL 48, which doesn't quite fit the usual image of a dash for Gretna.

'Saturday last' seems to work out at June 14, 1834. PL and Mary married at St Michael's on June 15. It was by licence rather than banns, and the witnesses were not family members. But, the Gretna idea seems to be more of a flight of fancy by the Herald than a flight of love!

The marriage is a happier story than the first two. PL and Mary had five children, and one while one died aged 19, one at 28 and one at 34, they all outlived their father.

Respectable times

Having given up as a corn merchant, PL settled down to life as a farmer and pillar of the community.

He is named in 1835 in connection with Bowness School, which was said (rather impressively) to have a library, globe, maps, quadrant, telescope, and maths instruments, and; mercantile accounts, navigation and astronomy on the curriculum.

In 1837, PL was the commissioner sorting out the 'inclosure' Act in Whitrigg, where he occupied land. He was the valuer for the enclosure of Whitrigg Marsh and High Pasture, in 1847, when he called a meeting for anyone claiming common rights at 'the house of John Peat' – ie the Steam Packet, at Port Carlisle.

Around this period, more than one person assigned their estate to PL in trust for their creditors, and he was named on several 'to let' adverts as the person to go to for details.

Polling records (no secret ballot back then) showed him voting for James Graham when he was still a Whig, but in 1844, he donated £1 to a memorial fund for William Lowther, the late Earl of Lonsdale and a Tory MP. Their connection had been professional, and may or may not also have been political.

PL was also a Poor Law guardian, a post he kept after an election in 1851 (as detailed in the chapter on Peter Irving, who came third).

He was accused, in 1847, of failing to pay the Poor Rate himself – £7 15s 7d. Summoned by the church wards and overseers acting for the parish, he said he objected to paying as he had advanced money for some orders of removal (ie of paupers to other parishes). In the end, it was ruled the rates hadn't been properly set in the first place, as they hadn't been properly signed.

Fish

As mentioned in the chapter on Jeffray Peat (1769-1836), in a court case in 1859, PL said he had been collecting fishing rents for the first, then second earls of Lonsdale since 1843.

However, in January 1852, the (pro-Whig, anti-Lowther) *Carlisle Journal* had published 'The Solway Fishing Case – a plain, unvarnished tale'. In it, a man called Thomas Percival claimed while PL had been collecting rents, the Lonsdale estate had known nothing about it and hadn't received the money!

The unvarnished tale is certainly a rambling one, Thomas Percival giving almost a minute-by-minute account of who (he claimed) did and said what and when.

The Journal tells us the account was written on a slate in Carlisle Gaol. It must have been a big slate!

Thomas Percival was a Bowness-born shoemaker who in 1851 was 28 and had a wife and two babies to provide for. He was in jail for debt because he had taken the Earl to court, in August 1851, for trespass, after the Earl's agents cut Tom's nets. The jury had found, in effect, that Lord Lonsdale had the rights to the shore, but not to the fishery. Tom couldn't pay the legal costs his lordship had incurred, namely £591 16s 7d, as his assets amounted to £7.

During the August hearing, PL had told the court he had been appointed by Lord Lonsdale, in 1833 or 1834, to look after 'the wreck' (flotsam and jetsam) from Drumburgh to Cardurnock. He said he'd received £8/£9 for collecting fishing rents, but had yet to be paid for looking after the wreck.

'Poor Tom' earned a lot of sympathy and was viewed as a martyr by those who believed the Lowthers shouldn't be charging fishing rents at all – either because locals had the right to fish the Solway from tradition, or because they disputed who owned the foreshore, the Lowthers or the Crown.

Others (in the pro-Tory, pro-Lowther *Carlisle Patriot*) thought it was better for someone to be able to charge fishing rents, as that person could then restrict the number of permits – and stop it being a free-for-all.

Brought before the courts on January 28, 1852, Tom was discharged, without opposition.

If PL sought to defend his reputation over the 'slate' accusations, I haven't found it.

As for poor Tom, it seems his experiences gave him a taste for the law and justice – for in 1861, he appears on the census as a police sergeant. He, wife Ruth and son Peter (baby Ann looks sadly to have died) had also moved 150 miles, to Runcorn, in Cheshire.

Assault and extortion

Whether the claims about PL and the fishing rents were libellous or true doesn't seem to be recorded. However, in June 1855 he was branded 'cowardly,' after being convicted of assaulting a woman called Elizabeth Ewart. From the 1851 census, she'd have been 52, living alone, and a farmer of three acres.

The story was that Elizabeth owned three cattle. which PL had locked in his shed, demanding she pay two shillings to release them.

A lad named Robert Poole, who had been herding them for Elizabeth, said the cattle hadn't been near PL's land till one pf PL's daughter (he thought Mary Ann) had driven them into their yard.

Elizabeth went to see PL, who demanded the 2s. When she said she didn't have it on her, he was said to have pushed her against the wall and hit her several times with a thick willow walking stick.

She told the court PL had threatened to knock her brains out, and showed the bench a very severe bruise on her left arm.

The clerk to court said PL had no right to charge her anything, as his place was not a pinfold and he had not sent her any notice that he had impounded her cattle.

The assault was proved, and PL was fined 10s and costs. Total £1 14s 2d, which he paid straight away.

It certainly didn't leave him repentant, for just a month later he was accused of extorting a sovereign from Miss Ewart for impounding a pony that had strayed – allegedly telling her that having been fined 34 shillings a few weeks earlier, he'd take a sovereign of it in that way. The case was adjourned and I've not found an outcome.

In 1857, a Thomas Rowlands sought damages from PL. Thomas had rented 20 acres from PL and put sheep and cattle on them.

He'd been hurt in a railway accident, and asked PL to see to them, but on his return, found they were in poor condition.

This was because PL had put someone else's bullocks to graze there and they had eaten the field bare. £16 4d damages sought, but the case was adjourned for counter-action – which doesn't seem to have been reported.

The final years

In 1861, PL was still at Bowness Hall, farming 400 acres, with his third wife Mary, their son John (24), daughter Margaret (21), a relation of Mary's called Thomas Collinson (15), and three farm servants

In 1862, he 'narrowly escaped being taken in' by swindler George Thurley, who bought potatoes from a bunch of farmers with spurious bills (cheques).

And then, aged around 76, he began to 'downsize'.

An advert in March 1862 offers Bowness Hall to let: the dwelling, outbuildings, 100 acres of arable, 60 acres of grazing land, and 240 of common or moss land – apply to PL the owner.

Ten months later, there's a stock and crop auction sale: 21 Galloway cattle, 10 horses, 20 grey-faced Highland ewes in lamb to a Leicester tup; a sow and pigs, ten stacks of grain, two of hay, growing turnips and potatoes, and all the husbandry and dairy utensils, the property of PL.

That seems a bit back to front, but in 1863, when he attended, with other farmers and gents of the district, a highway meeting at Burgh about the new Highway Act, which they weren't keen on, he was described as 'of Bowness Hall'.

And that, on June 27, 1865, is where PL died.

His will makes no mention of his son John. He was a landowner in Bowness in 1871 (he died that summer), but Bowness Hall was occupied by a family called Little.

PL left his wife Mary £2,000 (to be divided between his daughters and their assignees after her death).

Mary was also left the stock, crop, husbandry utensils, household furniture, linen, plates, china, books, monies, goods, etc. Again, after her death, these were to be divided between daughters Jane Rhoda Tully, Margaret Collinson Lawson, Mary Ann Lawson, and Elizabeth Lawson.

Mary lived on a further 23 years, dying at 19 Victoria Place, Carlisle, in 1888. Her estate was then valued at £11,100.

Pattinson Lawson is also named on this family memorial

21

Westfield House

A confusion of Pattinsons – one of whom married a Port Carlisle Peat

 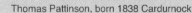

Jane Peat, born 1844 Port Carlisle   married   Thomas Pattinson, born 1838 Cardurnock

JUST round the corner, relatively speaking, from Port Carlisle is Westfield House farm. Its history – or rather, that of its bygone occupants – has long caused me confusion.

After a lot of effort and years of digging, I still haven't cracked it all. But, I have uncovered a few 'stories'.

Which, as fits a confusing situation, I will tell in reverse.

And if you can read it without getting a headache, it does include some human interest stories, amid the lists of names and dates.

John Pattinson, born about 1803, died 1873

Will: 1873. John Pattinson of Westfield House, farmer.

Son William gets the furniture, plate, china, glass, linen, books, prints, pictures and other household effects.

Grand-daughter Isabella (Will's daughter) gets a dozen silver teaspoons, 'to and for her own use.'

All farming stock, crop, husbandry and dairy utensils to be split equally between John's three sons: Thomas, William and John.

Son William (1841-1929) is confusing because of his grave at St Michael's, Bowness. With him are buried his two wives, Margaret (née Holmes, d. 1876 Low Town House) and Grace (née Gourlay, d 1928 Low Town House), and his brother John (d 1923, Port Carlisle). But one the other side are more Pattinsons, from Longcroft – and I have no idea why, as there's no apparent connection between the two families.

Meanwhile, brother John's life between 1871 (at Westfield, with his father) and 1901 & 1911 (at Easton, with William and Grace) is a bit of a blank. 1901 says he's a widower. In 1881, he looks to have been at Drumburgh with a wife and two children, but I can't find him in 1891.

Long before antibiotics

Son Thomas (1838-1895) married (Wigton Register Office, April 10, 1869) Jane Peat, of Kirkland House. She was the daughter of John Peat and Elizabeth (née Simpson), who has her own chapter in this book.

Their marriage certificate describes Thomas as a farmer, 'of Whitefield House' (sic).

Thomas moved into Kirkland House, with the Peats. Daughter Isabella arrived five months later, followed by Elizabeth in June 1871, when they were still at Kirkland.

Elizabeth died just under four years later and was listed on a Peat grave (her great-grandparents', Jeffray and Ann) as being 'of Glasson'.

Thomas and Jane are supposed (family story) to have had one of the cottages alongside the Steam Packet (Hesket House), at Port Carlisle, converted by Jane's father. However, sources put them at Anthorn in 1879, and at Low Town House in 1881 (a family called Sibson were then at Westfield). Then back at Kirkland House from 1884 – although the Peats had left Kirkland by 1879, and the Littledales were there on the 1881 census.

None of this sounds much like a 'story' – but how he died has been passed down the family.

Thomas was all set to take up Bulls Head farm at Plumpton, when he was scratched or nipped on the hand, playing with a collie puppy. It seemed nothing at the time – as a farmer, he was no doubt used to far worse. But, he contracted blood poisoning, which spread through his body, killing him on January 30, 1895 – at Kirkland House.

Confusingly, a newspaper obituary says he'd given up his farm 'at Westfield House', to move to Plumpton at Candlemas.

Rewind to a drowning

John Pattinson (1803-1873) hailed from Cardurnock. His wife Isabella was born around 1806 in Scotland (her maiden name may have been Mattinson).

She died on January 11, 1869, at Westfield House, aged 63, in puzzling circumstances.

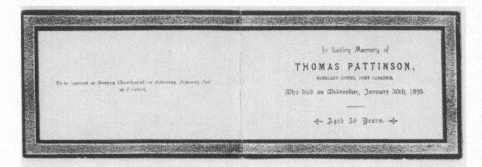

In Loving Memory of

THOMAS PATTINSON,

KIRKLAND HOUSE, PORT CARLISLE

Who died on Wednesday, January 30th, 1895.

✦ Aged 56 Years. ✦

To be interred at Bowness Churchyard on Saturday, February 2nd at 2 o'clock.

Her death certificate says she was found dead, accidentally drowned, in a pond. While intoxicated.

The certificate says 'Whitefield House' again, instead of Westfield. It also says there was an inquest on January 13, but there's no record of it at Carlisle Archives, nor in any newspaper I've searched either on the British Newspaper Archive, or scrolling through yards of microfilm in Carlisle Library.

Westfield House, a coincidence?

What bugged me for years was whether John (1803) was related to the Pattinsons who were at Westfield House from the 1700s.

The answer is 'probably no'. But, it took a lot of work to piece things together.

John hailed from Cardurnock, the son of another John (about 1769-November 19, 1813) and Sarah (née Blackburn, about 1768-June 24, 1848).

John (1803) was an elector of Cardurnock in 1837, a yeoman there in 1839, and a farmer there until after the 1861 census.

He owned the farm, which ran to around 60 acres. He put it up for auction in 1859, changed his mind for some reason and cancelled the sale. Then put it back up for sale (or rent, if not sold) in 1862.

1862 was when Westfield House was advertised to let (with 118 acres). He was at Westfield for sure by 1867, when he gave evidence in the fishing inquiry (*see the chapter on fishing*).

1871: Westfield House. John Pattinson, widower, farmer 144 acres. Son William, married, 29, son John, unmarried 27. Daughter-in-law Margaret, 25, housekeeper; grand-daughter Isabella, 4; grand-daughter Sarah 2; grand-daughter Abigail, 1. A female farm servant, and Jane Holmes, visitor, 8, born Bowness (likely a relation of Margaret).

So, who were the pre-1862 Westfield House Pattinsons?

Simon begat Simon...

In 1730, a Simon Pattinson, of Easton, left lands at Easton and Drumburgh to son Thomas. There was a Simon baptised at Bowness in 1686 to a John, and two in 1670 (one to a Simon, one to a John). And the 1641/42 Protestations (of loyalty to the Anglican church) have a Simon of Cardurnock, and one at Drumburgh (with a George, a Rowland and two Roberts).

It gets a bit clearer after Thomas, when we reach:

Simon, b 1732, died 1788 Westfield House, buried at St Michael's.

Westfield went to his son Thomas, born 1767, died 1833, who was among a long list of people in 1819 protesting over the attacks on freedom of the press and democracy and the general fall-out from the Peterloo Massacre.

Westfield then went to his son John. Which is where it gets more complex.

John Pattinson, born 1797, died 1844

John married, in 1831, Ann Sanderson. She was born about 1811. They had three children: Thomas, born in 1832; John, born in 1839, died aged four, and: Ann, born in 1843.

In 1841, they were at Westfield (except Ann who hadn't been born yet, obviously), with John's widowed mother (another Ann) and two servants.

Sadly, John died at Westfield, on December 13, 1844, aged just 47, 'much respected.'

His will left everything to his wife, and thence to their son Thomas – who was then still a child.

As life turned out, widowed Ann was to complicate things by remarrying, and Thomas was to complicate things by dying young.

On January 13, 1848, Mrs Pattinson of Westfield House, near Port Carlisle, married Jeremiah Sharp, yeoman, of Glasson. He was a widower twenty years older than her with (I think) seven children. He and Ann went on to have two more.

Jeremiah moved to Westfield House, rather than Ann moving in with him – but he still kept the house and land at Glasson.

The 1851 census shows Westfield House: Jeremiah Sharp, 62, Ann 42, her children Thomas Pattinson, mariner, 19 and Ann Pattinson, 9, their son William Sharp, 1 and daughter Elizabeth Sharp, one week. Plus a visitor and a servant.

Thomas Pattinson the young mariner was to die just seven years later, aged 26. His father's will doesn't specify anything of the sort, but it would seem that when his mother remarried, Westfield House passed to him (or at least when he turned 21, in 1853). It also seems he was prepared for his early death, as he had – in 1853 – written a will.

In it, he says he owns estate inherited through his mother. If he dies without issue, his sister Ann is to get Westfield House. If she dies without issue, his half-brother and half-sister, William and Elizabeth Sharpe, are to get Westfield House.

So, in 1858, Westfield House legally passes to sister Ann. Who in 1860 marries Christopher Topping... so that in 1861, those living at Westfield are: Jeremiah Sharp, wife Ann, 50... her daughter Ann and husband Christopher Topping, son William Sharpe 12, daughter Elizabeth Sharp, 10, (Jeremiah's) granddaughter Mary Dalton, and a general servant Catherine McKinzie, 16, great-granddaughter of Jeffray Peat and Ann (née Lawson).

Another tragedy

If you've made sense of that… months later, Jeremiah was 'missing, presumed dead'.

He had been a keen hunter all his life and went out on December 2, 1861, to shoot fowl on the Solway. He sailed over to the 'Scotch' side – and never returned. He was caught by a strong tide and his small boat capsized. The boat was later cast ashore, but his body was never recovered. His son John put adverts in the press, offering a £5 reward to anyone finding his father – with the detail that his initials, JS, would be found on the inside of his left arm, near his elbow.

Newspaper coverage says he'd taken on Westfield House with his second marriage, but had kept his own house and land at Glasson as well.

Jeremiah's will left his widow Ann the furniture, china, glass, linen, woollen, and household goods. Their children William and Betty Sharp got the rest of the Westfield House personal estate (ie stock, crop, husbandry utensils), to be sold for cash for them as they were under 21.

His landed estate at Glasson was to be sold and proceeds divided into nine. William and Betty got get1.5 share each. Other children to get one share each were: John, Jonathan, Mary, Ann Brown (wife of Thomas), Esther Dalton (widow of Joseph), Jane White (widow of John).

A notice duly appeared, saying the house and 39 acres at Glasson would be sold by auction on November 28.

And Westfield House?

1862, Friday, September 19. To let and be entered upon at Candlemas next, all that farm situated at West-Field House, Port Carlisle, consisting of 118 acres of land, nearly in a ring fence, and in a state of cultivation, being in the hands of the owners during the last century.

So, with Ann widowed again, and Westfield belonging to her daughter Ann and her husband Christopher Topping, who had their own place, it was rented out.

And by 1867, for sure, it was being rented by John (1803) and Isabella Pattinson. With John, in a yet another fishing case, telling a court hearing: 1867. "I am tenant to Mrs Ann Pattinson, of Westfield House."

Well, not quite! Ann senior was Ann Sharp, her daughter was Ann Topping.

The former, in 1871, is listed as living in Port Carlisle with her son William Sharp, 21, an unmarried fisherman. Of course, it can't be that simple. They are followed by a married Betsey Sharp, 32, a mariner's wife, and her children, who are seven, three, and one. Who clearly can't be William's family (he's single, and only 21!).

As for Westfield House… in 1871, it was occupied by John Pattinson (1803), as stated above.

In 1881 and 1891, a family called Sibson were there (*they appear in a previous chapter*).

By 1901 (and in 1911), it reverted to the 'centuries-old' Pattinson line, being occupied by Christopher and Ann Topping.

Westfield House October 12th 1815

Mr Lumly

Sir last time I seed you at Carlisle I spoke to you respecting cleaning the Drain along the Road side in the West Moss, you told me that the Publick Drains was to be cleand by the publick untill the common was a Warded in the presence of John Hodgson, who was an acting Person under you — I frequently spoke to him concerning cleaning it, but never got any satisfaction— last year I had a part of the Crop entirely wasted— I have part of the West moss under management for Wheat or Rye but it will be of no use to sow it untill the Drain be cleard— should the Drain not be to be cleand by the Publick I wish you would inform me Immediately for the rest hereof & I will endeavour to cause it to be done—

your compliance to the above will greatly oblige

Your most Obedt. Humbl Servant

Thos. Pattinson

A letter written in 1815 from Thomas Pattinson of Westfield House, to Lord Lonsdale's agent

22

And finally...

A few explanations

The author

Firstly, this book has been written under the pen name I use for my history blog, *Cumbrian Characters,* which you can find at www.crimesofthecenturies.com

Secondly, as an 'outsider,' I cannot claim any special knowledge of Port Carlisle or its surrounds – any more than historians who write about ancient Rome!

What I can claim is that at least seven generations of my family (that I can 100 per cent confirm) were baptised at/lived in Bowness parish. We are talking back to 1660, with unconfirmed 'possibles' going back to a death in 1594. The Solway coast is in my DNA.

Duplication

Because I haven't written everything in a linear, chronological order (I think that would be very dull), there is some overlap of content in chapters.

For instance, a chapter about one individual may contain information about his parents, who feature in another chapter.

In the hope of avoiding confusion, I have therefore repeated some of the biographical details about those people, so it is clearer just who/which generation I am talking about, and how the families fitted together.

Name variations

Spelling in bygone days was not always consistent. 'Can't go wrong' forenames names like John and Mary were fine, even when the bearers were illiterate. But some forenames and a lot of surnames were inconsistent – sometimes, for example it was a vicar's assumption of how a name should be spelled.

Thus, for example, there's a Mary who appears on one certificate as Blenkinsop and another as Blenkinship.

And while almost every generation of Peats had a Jeff, it could be (and was) spelled Jeffray/Jeffery/Jeffrey/Jeffry/Geoffrey – sometimes for the same person.

I've tried to go with the variation that appears most often, but haven't standardised the spelling for all mentions.

Further, because Christian names ran in families, it can get confusing as to which individual is being referred to. Thus, I have referred to one Jeff as 'junior,' and thereafter 'JJ'. While to distinguish Peter John Irving from his father Peter, I have abbreviated him to 'PJ'. It's also warmer than being formal about people who were not just names and dates in parish registers, but living, breathing, hoping, dreaming, happy, sad individuals.

Sources

In all my family history and other research, I never fully trust anything that isn't backed up by at least two sources – eg, a census return backed up by a birth certificate. However, I've never found recording the sources especially interesting, and in the early days, I really didn't care as I had no need to 'prove' things to anyone but myself. If I put something on my family tree, I KNEW that I'd verified it carefully.

Likewise, when writing this book, I'd have found it tedious and time-consuming to annotate every paragraph with a source. It would also make for a lot of numerical clutter in the text – and honestly, does anyone ever read the pages of source notes at the end of a book anyway?

Readers can be assured that I have only included information I have either verified, found on credible sources, or found on sources that cannot be verified but can reasonably be taken on a deal of trust – ie contemporary newspaper reports.

Key sources of information:

- The *Carlisle Journal* and *Carlisle Patriot*, and other newspapers (mostly – but far from entirely – via the excellent British Newspaper Archive's online service).

- Carlisle Archives

- Carlisle Library

- Census returns, wills, parish registers, birth/marriage/death certificates, and;

- St Michael's Church, Bowness-on-Solway, gravestones

Photographs

While I am not especially precious about my own photos, most of the photos in this book ARE mine

and it would be nice to be asked before anyone copies them.

I certainly respect copyright and have only used old images that are either mine (family album) or are from old postcards.

Should anyone hold the copyright to these, I will gladly remove the image from all future copies. On which topic...

Amendments

Finally, the aim of this book has been to share information I've found from research with anyone else who might be interested.

I have chosen the self-publishing route as this means it can easily be amended at any time – no incorrect copies sitting on shop shelves.

Should anyone wish to suggest amendments, they can do so via the 'contact us' page of:

www.crimesofthecenturies.com

Where you can also read an assortment of other Cumbria-related history articles.

Made in United States
Orlando, FL
03 June 2024

47479368R00083